The Third Way

The Third Way

India's Revolutionary Approach to Data Governance

Rahul Matthan

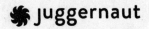

JUGGERNAUT BOOKS
C-I-128, First Floor, Sangam Vihar, Near Holi Chowk,
New Delhi 110080, India

First published by Juggernaut Books 2023

10 9 8 7 6 5 4 3 2 1

P-ISBN: 9789353452636
E-ISBN: 9789353451851

Illustrations by Priya Patil

Typeset in Adobe Caslon Pro by R. Ajith Kumar, Noida

Printed at Thomson Press India Ltd

For Appa

Contents

Contents

Terminology and Notes

Data protection regulations in almost every country follow a standard naming convention for the different parties concerned. The individual whose personal data has been collected is usually called the data subject, the entity that has either collected it or has effective control over it post collection is called the data controller, and any entity that performs any actions on the data (collection or any other form of processing) on behalf of the data controller is referred to as the data processor.

However, when Justice B.N. Srikrishna was tasked with drawing up a new regulatory framework for data protection in India, one of the first things he did was change this naming convention. The last time Indians were anyone's subjects, he said, was when the queen of England ruled India. And so, to underscore the central importance of the individual in data protection, the data subject is referred to, in India, as the data principal. Extending this principle even further, the data controller is referred to as the data fiduciary since it holds the data principal's personal data in trust.

In this book, I have used Justice Srikrishna's terminology, retaining the terms data principal and data fiduciary when referring to entities in the context of their data protection rights and obligations. If you are more accustomed to European terminology, kindly adjust your frame of reference appropriately.

I've always been irritated by books where footnotes take up half the page. Or where they are piled up at the end – leaving the reader feeling even though they have reached the end, they have not read all the author has to say.

Notes to text, in my mind, should be entirely optional – available to readers who want to go deeper – and not unnecessarily add to the bulk of the book. It is for that reason that this book has neither footnotes nor endnotes. For readers who want access to sources or additional material, that material is available at www.thethirdway.in.

Introduction

In 2008, less than one in twenty-five Indians had a verifiable identity. Just about 17 per cent had a bank account and only 15 per cent used digital payments. However, by 2018, almost every one of the 1.4 billion citizens of the country had a digital identity; over 80 per cent had a bank account and 68 per cent of all payments were digital. According to the World Bank, between 2014 and 2017, one of every two new bank accounts opened in the world was in India. In December 2022 alone, 8 billion digital payment transactions were processed in India.

This dramatic transformation can be directly attributed to the digital public infrastructure (DPI) that India has built, one layer at a time, for the last fifteen years. The resulting ecosystem represents a unique approach to solving societal problems by using powerful digital ecosystems built using open, interoperable architecture for public benefit. These ecosystems have evolved across a range of different sectors – from financial services to healthcare – and taken together, offer services ranging from identity and credentials to payments and credit. Thanks to the widespread penetration of mobile data, these are accessible to everyone, anywhere and at any time.

The transformation this has wrought across Indian society has had powerful ripple effects throughout the economy. While affluent sections of society could always access services like these (they already had verifiable identities, bank accounts and credit cards for digital transactions), the deployment of these systems at scale has significantly benefitted the poor and the marginalized, allowing them to significantly better their lives.

All the literature on the subject has, so far, positioned India's DPI as a digital transformation story, one that describes how India, through an ingenious use of digital technology systems, has been able to solve intractable societal problems with an efficiency and economy that have helped it leapfrog several stages in its economic development journey. These stories focus on the technology India has built, its design, its features and the outcomes it has achieved.

However, there is more to India's DPI story than simply the digital transformation it has wrought. Contained within these digital systems is a robust data governance framework that operates by embedding legal and regulatory objectives directly into code. This means that instead of looking to impose obligations through the enforcement of laws, compliance can be achieved by getting participants to use these ecosystems. This gives the regulators who manage the protocols and specifications on which these systems function direct control and, often, the ability to influence policy outcomes in real time.

This is a brand-new approach to data governance, one that represents a powerful new alternative to how the world has traditionally achieved regulatory objectives.

There are, broadly speaking, three actors in a digital ecosystem: market participants who use it to provide and receive services; regulators who establish the rules of the road, stipulating what can and cannot be done; and technology providers who build the applications, protocols and digital infrastructure that define the contours of the ecosystem. A well-functioning digital ecosystem allows each of these actors to operate at full potential. This is the role of governance.

This book looks at India's DPI from a governance lens. It describes how, in the hands of a thoughtful regulator, technology can be used to further policy goals. It describes how legal principles could be embedded directly into the fabric of the infrastructure so that the mere act of participating in the ecosystem guarantees compliance. It also describes how, by carefully arraying competing interests against one another, it might be possible to use the incentives that drive these different actors to achieve the stated objectives.

I will make my argument in three stages.

I will first discuss the challenges of data governance in the age of the internet, examining the problems that have arisen because of how data has insinuated itself into every aspect of modern society and the many legal and regulatory issues that regulators today have to deal with as a result. To do this justice, we will need to understand the history of computer and data technology, why it was created and what it has metamorphosed into.

We will reflect on how these new technologies have benefitted us and the harms that we now need to contend with. This will allow us to appreciate the need for data governance and the fine line that regulations need to walk between limiting what these technologies can be used for and ensuring that we can take full advantage of all they offer. In the process, we will examine the two distinct approaches to regulation prevalent today and why we need an alternative.

We will then discuss the range of solutions that comprise the entirety of India's DPI. Since it is beyond the scope of this book to provide a comprehensive listing of all the different elements of India's DPI stack, we will take a whirlwind tour of a representative sampling. I have found it helpful to organize DPI in India according to the different stages of maturity that they describe.

When countries start on their DPI journey, they design the DPI to provide citizens with *access* to the DPI ecosystem. At this stage of the maturity journey, DPI typically consists of digital identity and verifiable credentials. Once these have been established, nations need to enable *engagement* among participants in the ecosystem. A wide variety of DPI makes this possible depending on the sectors to which they are applied. The most common examples of this are the fast payments systems that countries establish to enable digital payments, but this category could also include solutions that enable commerce, logistics, education and healthcare outcomes.

It is only after the population has been engaged in the digital ecosystem for some time that it can graduate to the next stage of maturity – *empowerment*. At this stage, the DPI is used to enable citizens to take advantage of the digital trails that they have laid down by establishing frameworks for consented data transfers that put them in control of how their data can be used within an ecosystem of service providers to offer opportunities over and above what is currently available to them.

In the final section, I will discuss how India's DPI approach can be used to address the challenges of data governance. I will argue that the design principles on which India's DPI has been built on can, in the hands of a thoughtful regulator, be used to effect policy outcomes by implicitly shaping how interactions take place within the ecosystem. Based on India's experience of operationalizing these networks, I will attempt to describe how it is possible to carefully align the incentives of various ecosystem participants to achieve desired outcomes, even though some of these outcomes might be inimical to the stated objective of these participants.

Finally, I will argue that it is possible to embed regulatory principles directly into the code of the technical infrastructure. I will do this by analysing India's Data Empowerment and Protection Architecture, which has implemented a consented data sharing framework by directly encoding data protection principles into its workflows.

Section 1

The Challenges
of Data Governance

The Data Revolution

'Any sufficiently advanced technology is indistinguishable from magic.'

– Arthur C. Clarke

By the year 2000, we were already a technologically advanced species. We had tamed much of the planet, dedicating vast tracts of land to generate food, effectively eliminating, or at least significantly mitigating, the scourge of famine for much of the rapidly increasing global population. We had conquered the great distances that separated us with powerful machines that cross the seas and skies in relative comfort and safety. A massive global communication infrastructure had made it a trivial matter to speak to people anywhere on the planet. As a result, the world, which used to be a vast and largely inaccessible place, had become much, much smaller.

And yet, all our achievements up to that point, remarkable as they were, were about to pale in significance compared to what humanity was going to achieve over the next two decades.

While we've had the internet for decades, there were at the turn of the twenty-first century only 400 million people using it, nearly half of whom lived in North America and Europe. Today,

9

that number is fast approaching 5 billion, with the vast majority of internet users accessing it from Asia.

In 2018, the total amount of data consumed in the world was 33 zettabytes ($33x10^{21}$ bytes). By 2020, that rose to 59 zettabytes, and it is anticipated to reach 175 zettabytes in 2025. But apart from the sheer size of the number, what it is being used for and how, has changed so radically that our past selves would have considered much of what we take for granted today to be fantastical.

A large part of this transformation has been driven by the growth of mobile data. At the turn of the century, there were just 740 million mobile phone subscriptions worldwide. Today, there are more mobile phones than there are people on the planet. By the end of 2021, 4.3 billion people were using the internet on their mobiles, even though 3.2 billion people living within the footprint of a mobile broadband network were still not using it. In India, where the overall teledensity is 84 per cent of the population (over 1.1 billion people), 82 per cent of that is due to wireless access. Of India's 840 million broadband subscribers, 805 million access it over wireless broadband.

Most of these subscribers use the internet for instant messaging, voice and video calling and watching free videos. The single largest online activity is instant messaging, with nearly 62 per cent of global mobile internet users using some form of it daily. There has been an uptick in other uses too, thanks in no small part to the coronavirus (COVID-19) pandemic. Today, 38 per cent of mobile internet users report that they use the mobile internet for education at least once a week, an increase of over 10 per cent compared to 2019. Around 21 per cent use it to manage their health and 14 per cent to order goods or services.

After communication, the second-most popular activity is watching videos. YouTube, on its own, accounts for 25 per cent of global mobile traffic, with creators uploading 500 hours of videos to the site every minute. Over 2.6 billion people worldwide use YouTube every month, and 467 million of them are in India. This is nearly double the number of users from the second-largest market, which is the United States at 246 million. T-Series, India's largest music label and movie studio, has the largest number of subscribers globally, with 245 million subscribers to its YouTube channel at the time of writing. Every day, people watch over a billion hours of video, with more than 70 per cent of them doing so on a mobile device (there are over 10 billion YouTube installs on Android devices).

We can, today, find videos on just about any topic online, from music videos and movies from every corner of the planet to historical footage, educational content, social commentary and memes. There exists such an abundance of choice that it is impossible for anyone to consume all that is on offer. As a result, access to knowledge has truly become unlimited. Anyone can benefit from the expertise of the greatest minds that ever existed by simply surfing on their mobile phones at next to no cost.

And yet, the internet is so much more than just a source of information. Thanks to the ever-increasing abundance of mobile bandwidth, cloud storage and real-time computing, the internet has enabled the development of powerful technologies that power much of our daily lives in magical ways, so much so that the world we inhabit today would have seemed fantastical to someone even just twenty-five years ago.

Getting Around

Take navigation, for example. There was once a time when we had to plan carefully before going somewhere, getting clear directions as to how to get there, knowing that if we made a mistake, we were sure to get lost. There were times that I have gone back without finding what I was looking for because there was no way to ask for directions and course correct when I was obviously in the wrong place. Today, we just whip out our mobile phones, punch in our destination and wait scant seconds until an app plots the two or three routes to our destination, no matter where on the planet it might be. We get into our vehicles and head to where we are going without even checking to see if the route we are headed down is the most efficient, confident in the knowledge that even while we are en route, the applications on our phones will be monitoring the traffic ahead of us and will inform us of alternate routes, should there be another way to get to our destination sooner.

Many of us don't even worry about active navigation anymore. If we want to go somewhere, we simply summon transport that can take us there, knowing that there is an application that will identify our current location, deliver a car and driver to our doorstep, ready to take us wherever we want to go. Chores like shopping have become a thing of the past. We no longer need to go to stores to pick up what we need. We can simply order things from the comfort of our homes, no matter whether we are picking it up from our local grocery store or a bespoke boutique halfway across the planet.

All this is possible because the mobile devices in our pockets are not just communication devices – they are powerful multifunctional computers. They contain sensors that can locate us precisely, no matter where on the planet we might be, allowing us to navigate and to be the targets of navigation. They have gyroscopes and accelerometers built in that can, from how they jiggle in our pocket, sense when we are going for a stroll and when we are working out. This is why we no longer fear new places, assured that anytime we head out to a new destination, our phones will tell us how to get to wherever we want to go.

We've come to take all this for granted, but none of this would have been possible without our ability to gather vast amounts of data and use it to generate valuable insights. The maps we use on our phones today were generated, for the most part, by harnessing inputs from an army of volunteers who used early versions of these maps and helped improve their accuracy by correcting mistakes and identifying points of interest. Even today, improvements in most map applications are user-generated. The route information, along with travel times and traffic predictions, are the result of real-time calculations carried out using live inputs from the hundreds and thousands of commuters using those roads at that very moment, comparing the speed at which they are currently travelling with the speed that the algorithm had indicated you would have to drive at to get to your destination in time.

Everything Is Smart

But many of us, not satisfied with this level of data-fication, have gone one step further and embraced wearables, a wide variety of different devices that can be worn on our person, tracking our physical parameters in real time, 24/7. These include smartwatches that, in addition to telling the time, track our heart rates, oxygen saturation and atrial fibrillation to know if we are cycling or swimming, whether we have had a fall, or are about to have a heart attack. We also have rings and chest straps that offer increasing levels of accuracy to help monitor our sleep or our athletic performances. And for those who want to hack their vitals, there are constant glucose monitors that collect a minute-by-minute record of blood glucose from interstitial fluid.

In much the same way, our homes are filling up with smart devices. Our televisions understand us when we speak to them and can curate content for us across a range of different channels, organizing them all into a video feed of what we most like to watch. Some are smart enough to understand which family member is watching and can reorganize the feed to that person's preferences. Various other smart devices participate in our daily lives: smart speakers play music for us, remind us of what we need to do and shop for us when the cupboard is bare; doorbells can identify who is at the door, allowing us to screen visitors; and a range of smart plugs, light bulbs and electronic utilities can switch themselves on and off autonomously to improve the energy efficiency of our homes and offices or to simply improve our mood. All these devices are internet-enabled and optimally intelligent, capable of carrying out simple workflows either by themselves or as part of a cloud-based solution. They typically use information they gather from us and our environs to offer a level of convenience and comfort that would have been unheard of even a decade ago.

But the benefits of modern technology are far greater than just the gadgets they have enabled. Our lives today are greatly enriched by the power of data that we can now aggregate in vast 'data lakes' in the cloud, which can be easily accessed and analysed. All the devices and gadgets we have surrounded ourselves with suck data from us, piping it into these massive data warehouses where they are pooled with similar data from others from all over the planet. Because of the sheer volume of these massive data sets and the number of data fields they comprise, it is possible to discern patterns in the data that would have otherwise remained invisible. The trends that emerge allow us to predict events with a degree of certainty that would have otherwise been impossible. We have learnt to use powerful algorithms to harness such data sets, training them to corral insights out of that data – typically products or services we may like to purchase and activities we might want to perform.

We also take for granted the algorithmic recommendations we receive, that nudge us to a particular course of action that might not have occurred to us without prompting. When we listen to music, we are offered suggestions about the next track and, more often than not, I find myself trying the algorithm's recommendations. When I finish reading a book, I get a variety of suggestions about my next good read, each as eclectic as the one I just read. When we're done with watching a movie, almost before the credits finish rolling, we are presented with suggestions as to what we might want to watch next. Little wonder that Netflix users are happy to follow the algorithm's recommendations over 80 per cent of the time.

Health and Wealth

There are numerous other ways in which data is used for our benefit that have nothing to do with the commercial applications most visible to us. Take health, for example. Thanks to the veritable explosion of wearable devices, many of us now have a longitudinal record of various health parameters collected at intervals of as short as a minute apart. If these are plotted on graphs and tied together, they provide us with trendlines offering insights about our health. A recent study found that data from wearables could be used to predict the onset of influenza-like illness up to a week before symptoms appeared by analysing changes in heart rate and sleep patterns – offering hope of a new kind of early warning system in the event of another pandemic.

Data has also helped scientists make significant breakthroughs in our understanding of the human genome. Thanks to dramatic improvements in computational power and processing capabilities, it has become much easier to sequence the human genome and decipher its meaning. Scientists can now identify specific genes that contribute to certain diseases more accurately and develop personalized treatments. CRISPR gene editing technology has made it possible for scientists to edit an individual's DNA, potentially curing genetic diseases and even preventing certain conditions from developing in the first place. For example, in an episode of my podcast *Ex Machina*, I tell the story of how advancements in these technologies offered a young boy in Bengaluru, India, the chance at life which would otherwise be cut short because of a genetic defect that had already put him into a wheelchair at a very young age.

Lenders can use data to get new insights into potential borrowers to help them better understand their ability to repay. Credit bureaus have been collecting information on borrowers for decades, using this data to build a credit history and a record of payment behaviour. But what is different is the range of new and often unexpected data sources that lenders can now reliably lean on to determine creditworthiness. Many of these alternative credit-scoring models can consider data about the actual transactions the borrower has undertaken or the regularity with which they pay their utility bills. The more sophisticated of these algorithms also draw insights from unlikely parameters such as whether a potential borrower types in capital letters or the average battery life on their phone. For people who don't have a traditional credit history – and no direct way to get one – these algorithms are a viable path into the formal economy. Given that in India, only 14 per cent of small businesses have access to credit, leading to an astounding $530 billion credit gap, there is almost no option but to find ways to use these unusual technological workarounds.

Teachers can use data to gain insights about their students to improve their educational outcomes. By collecting information about the performance of their students across a range of different parameters, they can build a more granular picture of each student's strengths and weaknesses. This, in turn, can help them re-orient their teaching methodology to help each student improve. For instance, if a school can analyse data about reading speed, fluency and comprehension, it can identify patterns that can accurately predict which students are most at risk of falling behind and design interventions early enough to help struggling students catch up.

We have traditionally hired for jobs based only on resumes and interviews, even though we know that these are, at best, poor predictors of how a candidate will perform in a given job. By studying data from various sources, recruitment agencies can get a more complete picture of a candidate's qualifications, experience and preferences. Recruitment agencies are increasingly collecting data on personality traits, work style and company culture to assess a candidate's fit for both the role and the organization. Google famously discovered that the most effective teams are those made up of people with diverse backgrounds and perspectives, leading to a fundamental shift in how the company hired.

Examples, thus, abound of how data at scale, harnessed to technology capable of processing it, can offer actionable insights across a range of different sectors. A couple of decades ago, even if this was not accessible at scale, technology had progressed to the point where these possibilities were beginning to reveal themselves.

But while it might have been possible for the more prescient among us to have anticipated many of these advances, the one thing no one would have even dreamed of was how artificial intelligence would come to transform our lives by doing things that rival the capability of human minds.

If there ever was a technology so advanced as to be indistinguishable from magic, it would, at the turn of the century, have been artificial intelligence (AI).

Machine Intelligence

It all started with text. And search engines.

When the internet exploded, it rapidly grew so large that it soon became impossible to find anything useful unless someone showed you where it was. Search engines capable of doing this well became the gateways to our internet experience. Success began to be defined by how well the algorithm could understand what humans meant when they typed a query. If they were going to give us the precise result we needed, they needed to first understand what we were looking for.

And so, the IT industry dedicated itself to refining search engine algorithms to solve this problem. Since all the world's search queries ran through their pipes, all they needed to do was process this information and apply probabilistic rankings to possible outcomes. Over time, they became preternaturally good at this, to the point where not only were search engines able to understand what we were thinking when we typed a query into the search field, they were also able to predict our question before we finished typing it. This autocomplete functionality in search soon spilled over to various other areas. Our SMS and instant messaging applications began suggesting short responses to the messages we received and our email programs, which were able to process the history of our correspondence, suggested more extended responses.

What started as a simple autocomplete functionality has, today, evolved into much, much more. Voice assistants that were long viewed as little more than gimmicks – novelty items that could set the alarm or tell you what the weather would be – are today an integral part of our lives. We use them to order groceries, control our smart homes and even carry out financial transactions. Where they previously struggled to understand anything other than English spoken in a Western accent, they now have no problem understanding not only English spoken in a wide range of accents but virtually every major language on the planet. The impact of this on accessibility alone is significant as people who only speak their mother tongue can now use technology that was previously beyond their reach.

AI can also now generate, from scratch, images and videos that are indistinguishable from those made by humans. One of my favourite pastimes is using AI algorithms like Midjourney to create high-quality images as illustrations for my writing, for no better reason than it is fun to see what the algorithm comes up with. I am very rarely disappointed. I know that similar capabilities exist in video creation and it is only a matter of time before I graduate to trying my hand at that. Now computer-generated imaging has become such an integral part of the movie industry today that it is impossible to tell real actors from those entirely generated by CGI. The ability to generate high-quality videos based solely on the text prompts of a creator will soon radically transform the industry. There is no better evidence of that possibility than *The Crow*, a short film generated entirely by text-to-video AI, which won the Jury Award at the Cannes Short Film Festival in 2022.

If all of this leads you to believe that the AI advances are of little use for anything more than entertainment, you need look no further than how it is transforming the field of medicine. Image recognition algorithms are being used with incredible success in radiology. When applied to analysing X-rays, CT scans and MRIs, these algorithms have proved capable of detecting abnormalities invisible to the human eye. They can detect and identify pulmonary nodules, colonic polyps and micro calcifications which indicate different forms of cancer. In the case of skin cancers, they can detect a wide variety of sizes, shades and textures of suspected lesions better than a trained dermatologist could, to the point where they are sometimes capable of characterizing a tumour as malignant.

AI algorithms can also be used in drug discovery to design and evaluate molecules in silico by reducing the number of potential candidates to more manageable numbers. Also, in instances where drugs initially developed to address a particular medical condition can be repurposed to treat another disease, these algorithms can be used to identify these possibilities. This is of relevance in poly pharmacology. There, deep learning algorithms can process information about the performance of drug candidates screened from a library of virtual compounds across multiple targets to identify a single drug that can simultaneously interact with multiple targets.

As impressive as AI has been so far, we are, at the time of this writing, on the brink of yet another transformation that promises to be even more dramatic. Over the past year or so, remarkable improvements in the capabilities of large language models (LLMs) have hinted at a new form of emergent 'intelligence' that can be deployed across a range of applications whose full scale and scope will only become evident over time. So powerful is the potential of this new technology that some of the brightest minds on the planet have called for a pause in its development out of the fear that it will lead to a SkyNet future and the genuine threat of unleashing malicious artificial general intelligence.

LLMs are computer algorithms designed to generate coherent and intelligent responses to queries in a human-like conversational manner. They are built on artificial neural networks that have typically been trained on massive data sets that allow them to learn language structure. LLMs can learn without being explicitly programmed. They can, therefore, continue to improve the more data they receive.

At their core, LLMs are not that different from the autocomplete technologies that started us down this path. They are designed to predict the probability of the next word in a sentence based on the previous words in the sentence, but they have mastered the technique to such an extent that they can autonomously generate tomes of text in a style that is often indistinguishable from a human author.

LLMs have the potential to revolutionize how we interact with technology and, in the process, with one another. One of the most significant benefits of LLMs is their potential to improve access to information. By analysing vast amounts of text, LLMs can create summaries and identify critical information, making it easier for individuals to access information quickly and efficiently. For example, in India, LLMs trained on an extensive database of government subsidies and benefits could engage with potential beneficiaries of these programmes through a conversational interface that allows them to query whether these benefits were applicable to them and if there were any ancillary schemes they could apply for. When integrated with real-time language translation capabilities, the power of AI to transform the lives of the poorest and most marginalized becomes immediately evident.

Trade-Offs

It is hard to argue against the fact that technology has benefitted humans immeasurably. Most of us have taken these data-driven technologies for granted, having forgotten what life was like without our digital accessories, almost assuming that the pace at which new technologies are born, develop and mature is as it always has been – and as it should be.

But despite these benefits, it is impossible to ignore that there is a price to pay for the privilege of using these technologies. More and more evidence demonstrates that all these incredible technologies, such integral parts of our lives today, have also been responsible for all manner of harm. While the problems they cause are rarely, if ever, evident when we first start to use them, over time, unwanted side effects of new technologies almost inevitably raise their ugly heads. So much so that many today argue that had we known all that we know today, we may never have embarked down this path in the first place.

We need to find a way to strike a balance between the harms and the benefits of digital technologies. We need to find a way to benefit from the value they offer while minimizing the harms that could arise. To do that, we need to have a handle on all that could go wrong, to understand the many ways in which the technologies we rely on affect us – both now and into the future – so that we can find ways to mitigate those consequences. But first we need to appreciate the many ways in which technology can cause us harm.

The Devil's in the Data

'Technology is a useful servant but a dangerous master.'
– Christian Lous Lange

In the late eighteenth century, Jeremy Bentham had a novel idea for incarceration. Instead of being arranged side-by-side, prisons should be redesigned to be circular, with individual cells arranged around a central observation tower. The prisoners would, at all times, be visible to the tower, but since they could not see into it, they would never know whether they were being watched. Since the inmates never knew when they were being watched, they would assume they were watched all the time and be more compliant. Bentham argued that this psychological pressure to conform was more effective than physical coercion.

He called his prison a panopticon and extensively promoted this revolutionary new idea in prison architecture, claiming that it could maximize control with minimal manpower. Despite his zealous advocacy, however, the British government never really implemented his design. His brother, Samuel Bentham, did incorporate some elements of the panopticon into his design of the Millbank Penitentiary in London, but apart from that, few prisons in Britain adopted it.

24

Elsewhere in the world, however, the concept had significantly more traction. In the United States, the Stateville Correctional Center in Illinois was notorious for its panopticon-inspired roundhouse. The Eastern State Penitentiary in Philadelphia modified Bentham's ideas to create a 'panopticon-rotunda' where solitary confinement and constant surveillance are de rigeur. In Cuba, the Presidio Modelo directly implements the panopticon design with five circular buildings, each housing up to 2,500 prisoners. Belgium's Prison Leuven Centraal and the Netherlands' Koepelgevangenis in Haarlem, Arnhem and Breda are among the most prominent European instances.

Since his ideas were primarily implemented on foreign soil, Bentham died without knowing whether his radical new approach to incarceration was everything he thought it would be. This was probably for the best – because it was not.

Prisoners incarcerated in panopticon-style prisons suffered debilitating psychological side effects that stayed with them long after being discharged. Rather than rehabilitating them as he had hoped they would, the panopticon ravaged the mental well-being of its inmates, in many instances driving them mad. Their loss of privacy lead to chronic stress, depression and mood disorders. The living arrangements fostered a sense of powerlessness and loss of autonomy. But above all, it stripped them of their individuality and dignity by reducing them to objects of observation in an inherently dehumanizing manner.

Humans are wired to respond to threats in their environment. The ever-present surveillance within the panopticon placed them in a constant state of alertness, a psychological phenomenon known as hypervigilance. Prolonged hypervigilance leads to anxiety disorders – restlessness, difficulty concentrating and disturbed sleep. Over time, it leads to paranoia and a chronic, pervasive distrust of others. The fact that they were under constant observation meant that they could never relax or let their guard down – that there was no moment when they could truly be themselves. And during their incarceration that destroyed them.

Most of us are not imprisoned under the permanent gaze of prison guards. Still, the technologies we depend on have immersed us in an environment of such constant supervision that we might as well be. The communication channels that are always available to us – our mobile phones, social media applications and over-the-top (OTT) messaging platforms – have made it incredibly simple to stay connected with anyone. But because these systems are entirely digital, they can also be intercepted. The cameras around us – in our phones and on the streets on which we walk – collect a constant feed of visual information about us and upload this content to the cloud in a never-ending stream of bits that can be stored and processed in myriad different ways. When this information is combined with modern advancements in image and facial recognition technology, it becomes possible for anyone with access to this data to actively monitor everyone – at every moment of the day.

We would like to believe that this is a relatively new phenomenon. That the digital surveillance we are subject to is the product of the modern internet and, had it not been for the proliferation of mobile technologies, we might never have been subject to this level of electronic oversight. But that is not entirely true. Since they were first created, computers have been designed to monitor, categorize and classify us. Everything that followed from there was just the natural consequence of that original objective.

Who Are You?

One of the earliest practical applications of computational technology was the 1890 United States Census. At the time, the US had received such a massive influx of immigrants that the nationwide census was taking an entire decade to complete. By the time one census was complete, it was time to start the next. Unless there were ways to speed this process up, the sheer volume of people being added to the population would overwhelm the purpose of the exercise.

There was, thus, a need to automate this process and Herman Hollerith was given that task. He broke up the process of data collection into two steps. He first reduced the data into a standard format and made sure that answers to his census questionnaire – age, sex, religion, occupation, place of birth, marital status, etc., – were digitized by getting census takers to punch holes in a card corresponding to the answers they had been given. He then fed each card into a machine that 'read' the information on it by pressing a set of electrical pins on the card. The pins that passed through the paper where holes had been punched completed an electrical circuit, while those that were stopped by the paper did not. In this manner, he could quickly aggregate data for each person with far more accuracy than if this was done manually.

While Hollerith's machines allowed the census to be completed with far greater efficiency than ever before, the real value was the level of analysis that was now possible. Data could be sliced and diced with incredible specificity, elevating the simple census into something altogether more powerful. By applying filters to the data, it was possible to find and isolate groups of people in specific categories, creating what Hollerith called, with some pride, 'a punch photograph of each person'.

From a current perspective, this doesn't sound very good. The fact that anyone has enough data about us to be able to build even a hazy image of all that defines us is a matter of grave concern. But this was the dawn of the information age. All that anyone was thinking was that without Hollerith's tabulating machines, it would have been impossible to bucket the hitherto undifferentiated populace into smaller sub-groups, allowing the state to better administer to their needs. By associating every citizen with relevant attributes – age, sex, religion, occupation, place of birth, marital status, criminal history, etc. – it was possible to group them more easily with others like them so that the services they were legitimately entitled to could be more easily provided.

The company that Hollerith founded was eventually folded into a computer business called International Business Machines – the company we know today as IBM. For much of its early existence, it was involved in projects that used machines to process vast volumes of information that had previously been compiled manually. Its clients were the great nations of the world that wanted to organize information about their people in previously impossible ways, categorizing them by a range of different criteria to make administration more efficient. The benefits were immediate and measurable.

This is probably why no one realized the problems that could result from the use of tabulating machines until it was too late. During World War II, these machines were used to identify Japanese Americans who were believed to be sympathetic to the country of their racial origin, with whom the US was now at war.

They helped locate this part of the population and identify their next of kin so that entire families could be rounded up and sent to internment camps. In Nazi Germany, these same machines were used to search through genealogical records of the populace to identify Jews so that they, too, could be gathered up and sent to concentration camps where many of them would die.

Tabulating machines made it possible to process vast amounts of information relatively quickly. They were, virtually from the moment of their creation, used on people, identifying them so that their governments could serve them better or single them out for differential treatment. One might argue that, from their very earliest designs, these devices were created for the precise purpose of knowing us better and, by extension, finding us like so many needles in the proverbial haystack when the state had reason to.

And if these machines were more powerful than the human tabulators before them, they would only grow more so when networked with each other.

The Power of the Network

The next step in the evolution of technology-enhanced surveillance was hastened into existence by the Cold War and the US government's desire to build a network of computers resilient enough to withstand a nuclear attack. Even as geopolitical tensions grew after World War II, they were exacerbated by the race to space between the two global superpowers.

Fearing Soviet superiority, the US put all its resources into developing technology to protect the country from a Soviet nuclear attack from space. This included building spy (and weather) satellites and developing ballistic missile technologies for defensive and offensive purposes. And since the mathematics of these endeavours was beyond human capability at the scale and speed that defensive measures demanded, there was an increased focus on developing more advanced computational abilities.

By then, computerization had already penetrated deep into the US defence establishment. But all the different departments had built their own computer systems, each with their own programming structure and designed to perform other specialized functions relevant to that department. As the Cold War progressed, the US government began to feel the inefficiency of having each defence system operate in its own silo. There was an urgent need for an effective command-and-control system to coordinate all the tasks carried out by every computer within the US defence department – from missile tracking to behavioural studies, voice communication and analysis of signal intelligence.

The Defense Advanced Research Projects Agency (DARPA), a special agency of the US Department of Defence, was tasked with getting this done. DARPA was responsible for developing much of the technology behind modern ballistic missiles as well as all the spy and weather satellites that dot the stratosphere today. But for the most part, DARPA's primary focus was on advancing the efficiency with which US defence departments used computer technology.

To get all the computer systems of the US government to communicate, they needed to speak the same language – a universal dialect of computers as it were – so that all machines, regardless of their form or function, could easily understand each other. Since so many of these systems were already deeply entrenched, it was impossible to retrofit. Instead, DARPA built a simple networking platform that had a few essential components that all of the many disparate military systems could use to share data.

To implement this, DARPA developed Interface Message Processors (IMPs), computers designed to only send and receive data. These dumb nodes had no other function except to check incoming data for errors and ensure that the received data was transmitted error-free to the next node in the network. Since this system had to be resilient enough to survive a nuclear attack, IMPs were designed to be optimally redundant. They were optimized to try and send data through multiple routes so that if any part of the network went down, there was always another pathway the data could flow through.

IMPs were the world's first internet routers that connected different computers so that they could share data regardless of make or model or the underlying purpose of the data. They pioneered the use of decentralized design, open protocols and modular architecture that came to characterize the internet. In the process, they turned the conventional wisdom of the time – that network topology had to be hierarchical, using top-down command-and-control structures to ensure control over all aspects of the ecosystem – on its head. Since every node in the DARPANET – the network of the DARPA – was as crucial as every other, the destruction of one, or even several nodes, had no impact on the overall stability of the network.

This is how the modern internet came to be – a truly decentralized network capable of being used by any computer hardware or software designed to share data and which, at the same time, was not subject to the control of any one country or commercial entity. So even though the internet was originally devised to connect defence technologies, it did not take long for it to be used for other purposes.

Surveillance as a Tool of War

During the Cold War, the US was also engaged not only in several minor wars but in peace efforts across various different conflicts. Many of these were not all-out wars but local, minor conflagrations where the US intervened to prevent their escalation into something with serious geopolitical consequences.

To achieve their objectives, the US defence establishments, as well as its diplomats, needed human intelligence – information that would allow them to better understand the people they were dealing with in Vietnam, Cambodia and Laos.

To this end, the US military initiated extensive studies on local populations in many places, deploying an army of anthropologists, political scientists, linguists and sociologists to carry out data-gathering exercises to better understand who they were fighting. These investigators were charged with understanding the enemy better – why these factions believed so sincerely in their cause, how come their morale was so high even when engaged in a losing battle, and what it would take to make a dent in that fervour. As a result, they conducted hundreds of interviews with prisoners of war, generating tens of thousands of pages of intelligence.

The volume of information generated in this manner during the US operations in Vietnam was too large to process manually. And so, DARPA initiated a top-secret mission called the Cambridge Project to digitize and analyse human intelligence received from the field, building a common operating system and a suite of programs tailored to implement this behavioural science mission. For the first time, all the different programs in the US defense establishment were networked so that they could be accessed from any computer with an DARPANET connection, creating an interconnected digital infrastructure capable of carrying out data mining and surveillance and making predictions.

This project resulted in the creation of some of the earliest networked intelligence databases in the world. Its long-term impact on networked surveillance was to serve as a training ground for a generation of data scientists who learnt, while working on the project, the art of data mining. By making it possible to carry out data analysis across a vast network of computers, DARPANET expanded Hollerith's original 'punch-photograph' vision of individuals into something much larger and more all-encompassing.

And it was not long before the technology originally developed to gather intelligence on foreign nationals was being used by the US administration to monitor its own people.

Looking Inwards

The late 1960s was a time of considerable civil unrest within the US. In the aftermath of the assassination of Martin Luther King Jr, riots spread across the country. A militant black activist movement and strident anti-war sentiment across college campuses fuelled a mood of rebellion. This led to over 3,00,000 people descending on Washington, D.C., in 1969 to take part in the largest anti-war protest in American history.

These events led the US administration to consider the real threat of domestic counterinsurgency within the United States. They believed that the protests were evidence of a communist conspiracy to breed unrest and overthrow the US government from within. Driven by the mortal fear of a civilian uprising, the government began to deploy the techniques it had perfected on foreign battlefields on its people.

The country's intelligence services actively engaged thousands of plainclothes agents to target various individuals – from priests to elected officials, civil rights groups to anti-war protesters – to identify everyone who might be sympathetic to the communist cause. All the information gathered through this process of domestic surveillance was encoded onto IBM punch cards and fed into networked computers that could process information across over a hundred different categories and spit out customized reports about targeted individuals.

At the same time, other parts of the US government were also rapidly digitizing their internal workings. The National Crime Information Centre, built by the Federal Bureau of Investigation, digitized information about arrest warrants, stolen vehicles, and property and gun registrations across all fifty states. By the mid-1970s, this system was accessible in police cars through keyboard terminals, allowing the immediate search and retrieval of information even as the patrol car was on the road.

In 1967, another centralized database was proposed so that data about income tax and arrest records, health data, military draft status, social security information and banking transactions could be accessed and combined to provide complete information about all citizens. This data was proposed to be associated with a unique number that would serve as that person's lifelong identification number.

As all these digital databases were established, care was taken to ensure that they could be linked via DARPANET so that the power of networks could be amplified by the power of the information contained in them. Since almost all of this took place behind the closed doors of various government departments, the general public had no clue that their data was being collected, combined and aggregated in one place. As a result, few even knew of the truly frightening possibilities that these databases raised.

In 1975, NBC correspondent Ford Rowan broke a story about the existence of a sophisticated computer communications network the military was using to spy on Americans. 'If you pay taxes or use a credit card,' he said, 'if you drive a car or have ever served in the military, if you've ever been arrested or even investigated by a police agency, if you've had major medical expenses or contributed to a national political party, there is information on you somewhere in some computer. Congress has always been afraid that computers, if all linked together, could turn the government into "big brother," with the computers making it dangerously easy to keep tabs on everyone. In 1968, it killed a proposal for a national data bank which would have held all the computer files on every American. Last year the Congress rejected Fednet a plan to hook together the computer files of various government agencies. But NBC News has learned that while Congress was voting down plans for big computer link-ups, the Defence Department was developing exactly that capability: the technology to connect virtually every computer.'

This news report – aired nearly half a century ago – raised concerns very similar to those we are dealing with today. It is hard to imagine how, after knowing the problems that could arise from networked data, we did nothing to stop it. Or, how the NBC report, which had anticipated all the issues we are struggling with to this day, was so thoroughly ignored that few even know of its existence.

There are enough lessons in our past to inform our future if only we take the time to learn from them. But we rarely do and so, history repeats itself. The ills we fear subside when a light is shone on them, and they lie dormant until they are roused from hibernation by some new and powerful catalytic force.

Privacy or National Security?

Within ten days of the September 11 terrorist attacks, the United States enacted The Patriot Act, a law that dramatically reduced restrictions on law enforcement agencies to gather intelligence within the US. So profoundly had the country been scarred by the worst attack on its sovereignty in living memory that citizens were willing to sacrifice the privacy rights and civil liberties that were fundamental to their way of life to defend themselves against the clear and present threat to national security. Few knew it at the time, but this would set in motion a race to develop the most aggressive surveillance tools mankind had ever built by taking advantage of the increasing digitization of society.

Most American states began leveraging data technologies to gather insights to serve as early warnings of future attacks. The Manhattan borough in New York City was most viscerally affected by the terrorist attack. As a result, a series of measures were initiated to use data from closed-circuit television cameras, license plate readers, facial recognition software and cell phone tracking to generate intelligence about people's movements, activities and associations. Today, these systems still collate data from over 9,000 private and public cameras and 500 license plate readers into a central command centre where it is processed to respond to searches for suspects driving certain types of cars or wearing clothes of a particular colour.

Similar measures were adopted by other law enforcement agencies across the US. Many deployed real-time facial recognition systems that could match still images against databases of known individuals. Others used technologies such as automatic gunshot detection systems (that can pinpoint the location and type of gunfire on city streets), 'stingray' cell site simulators (which can siphon data off mobile phones as law enforcement officers drive by the homes from where these calls are being made) and sophisticated social media profiling (that trawls through online activity to obtain early warning indications of illegal behaviour).

In 2013, former National Security Agency (NSA) contractor Edward Snowden leaked classified information about the true nature and extent of NSA's surveillance activities. The leaks revealed that the US government, taking advantage of its centrality in the global exchange of data, was collecting vast amounts of data on millions of people, including their phone calls, emails and internet activity, and that it was sharing this data with friendly governments, including the United Kingdom and Australia. This data was being collected from several different sources. This included data directly sourced from the American Big Tech companies including Google, Facebook and Microsoft, from the undersea cables that carry global international communications traffic, from email, chat and file-sharing services, and from the internet traffic records managed by companies registered in the United States.

The Snowden revelations reverberated across the world as everyone realized just how exposed they were to surveillance. The conversations they believed they were having in private were easily intercepted. All the services they relied upon for everyday activities – email, instant messaging and voice calls – had backdoors that could be tapped. But while Snowden's data leak exposed the shenanigans of the US government, halfway across the world, state surveillance scaled heights that were unimaginable in the paranoid Western world.

Surveillance in China

While the NSA is, at least ostensibly, focused on collecting data to protect the country from external risks, surveillance in China is oriented inwards. It is aimed at providing the state the tools it needs to better control its large population. Using the technologies first developed in the West, China has enhanced them into fine-grained tools capable of extracting all manner of insights from the personal data of its people.

China's Golden Shield Project is best known for the massive firewall, dubbed the Great Firewall of China, that it operates to moderate the internet being accessed in China, preventing people from being presented with content that the government considers unsuitable. It also blocks access to all the major social media websites that do not agree to provide government censors the level of access that they demand. What is not as well known is that the Golden Shield Project also connects police bureaus around the country to a national identity database of every adult in the country, setting up, in the process, a surveillance system that can track everyone in the country as they go about their daily lives.

As a result, mass surveillance in China is instantaneous. This is perhaps most evident in Xinjiang, a province to the northwest of China that is home to the Uyghurs, a Muslim minority in mainland China that has been subject to increasing levels of persecution for decades. To keep the Uyghurs in check, law enforcement authorities in the region have taken increasingly intrusive measures to track them. They collect blood, voice and fingerprint samples from suspects. This enables them to identify Uyghurs from their genetic material, overheard conversations and any biometric trails they may leave. They photograph Uyghurs using special 3D cameras that capture their features from every direction to be able to identify them from any angle. As a result, there is nowhere they can go where they are not being observed.

Elsewhere in China, cameras and sensors help improve the lives of residents. An AI platform in Hangzhou called the City Brain augments governance in various ways. By optimizing traffic signals in real time, traffic congestion can dynamically be managed to allow first responders to get to the scene of an accident faster than anywhere else on the planet. A ubiquitous network of cameras in the city has allowed it to drastically reduce incidents of child abduction in its more affluent neighbourhoods.

But over time, even in Hangzhou, the ever-vigilant City Eye cameras were used to identify more and more minor violations – cars parked illegally or deliveries blocking the footpath, incidents that were flagged not because they were crimes but rather indicators of a lack of conformity to China's social values. Behaviour that the government was keen to correct. Eventually, this gave rise to the most aggressive attempt by a country to shape the conduct of its subjects through the coercive use of technology.

On 14 June 2014, the Chinese government unveiled its Social Credit System, a system designed to shape social behaviour using incentives that would 'allow the trustworthy to roam everywhere while making it hard for the discredited to take a single step'. It was designed to collect information about people who violated 'social morality, business ethics, honesty, and integrity' and to actively disincentivize such behaviour. Passengers who abused flight attendants would find themselves on no-fly lists, not just for that airline but for every airline. Anyone who failed to make payments on their loans or credit card bills would be ineligible to apply for certain types of jobs or travel. Authors whose posts on social media posts were critical of the government would have their internet broadband speeds drastically reduced and be denied public services.

The list of socially unacceptable behaviour came to include increasingly minor offences from evading subway fares, cheating on tests and failing to send children to school, to refusing to leave the hospital after being released or taking someone's seat on the train. Citizens were given aggregate scores on parameters across a range of social interactions, all of which were reduced to a single number representing the extent to which they conformed to the values of the state in order. When these blacklists were interlinked across a range of adjacent services, it created massive meta-lists of transgressors that were used to determine, a la *Black Mirror*, the extent to which they would be rewarded or punished. Citizens with a high social credit score were entitled to a range of benefits: lower interest on loans, priority access to housing and jobs, and faster travel through airports and train stations. Those with a low score were penalized: they were denied loans they would otherwise have been eligible for and placed at the bottom of the list of citizens entitled to apply for coveted Schengen visas.

Public–Private Surveillance

While it is true that surveillance in China is driven by the government, it would not be possible without the active involvement of China's powerful private sector. Chinese technology companies are unique in their symbiotic relationships with the state. They were actively nurtured by the Chinese government behind the Great Firewall of China to serve as domestic alternatives to the US-based internet giants such as Google, Facebook and Amazon. Apart from a vast captive market, they received a range of commercial benefits that allowed them to grow into the world's largest tech companies. As long as they obeyed the state's orders, these companies were left to their own devices and allowed to build their path to profit, leveraging data in ways impermissible in the West.

This allowed Chinese Big Tech to accumulate extraordinary amounts of data about their users – their online activity, physical location and interactions with those around them. They began to analyse this data using sophisticated algorithms designed to identify behavioural patterns that predict future actions to achieve objectives aligned with the interests of the state. For example, the underlying idea behind China's social credit framework was put into practice by the Ant Group (Alibaba's financial services arm) through its Sesame Credit system. This system used the social behaviour data of its customers to determine the benefits they were entitled to across the vast portfolio of the Alibaba empire.

Even though they originally started out providing different

services, the Chinese internet giants converged in the digital payments ecosystem. Today, nearly everyone in every city and village in China uses payment technology from one of the two biggest Chinese Big Tech companies, AliPay and WeChat, for everything they do – be it buying groceries from a street market or investing in the stock market. In 2020 alone, more than 123 billion transactions worth US$67.5 trillion took place on these platforms. This is eleven times the total payment volumes of MasterCard for the same year.

Money is an excellent proxy for much of our social lives. All this transaction data offered these companies the ideal vantage point from which to analyse their customers and build profiles for them. Jack Ma, the erstwhile swashbuckling head of Alibaba, said it best: 'Whoever owns enough data and computing ability can predict problems, predict the future, and judge the future.'

While Chinese companies might be the current masters of the art of data collection, their techniques are based on methods invented in the West. US companies recognized the value in harvesting data long before the internet, big data and cloud computing made it the powerful commodity it is.

The airline industry was one of the earliest industries to tap into the power of data. American Airlines built a registration and booking system called SABRE based on the US early warning air defence system. SABRE has since been hived off into a separate entity that is now the world's largest travel booking company.

It was not long before other industries followed suit. Banks and financial institutions were early to adopt computerization, focusing initially on their core banking operations but following up with online banking and an increasingly digital user experience. Hospitals and medical establishments built large enterprise solutions to track patients and their procedures, as did the hotel, transportation and retail commerce sectors.

These private systems collected as much (if not more) information about their users as the government systems did. No one questioned the appropriateness of this widespread data collection or worried about its harmful side effects. On the contrary, the fact that businesses were taking the trouble to retain information about customer preferences and past purchases was often seen as a valuable service, a sign that they cared about their customers enough to want to know what they liked, to serve them better.

American Airlines was the first to convert its data advantage into profit, offering computerized bookings at a speed its competitors could not match. Hospitals that had past medical records of a patient began to use them as leverage to encourage patients to keep returning to their facilities for other ailments, going so far as to make it extremely difficult for patients to extract their medical records if they wanted to go to another establishment. Businesses of all hues implemented loyalty programmes offering customers discounts, access to special services and a range of other benefits for higher spends. Customers believed that they were being rewarded for being loyal when, in fact, their continued participation in these programmes only offered the companies access to more and more data about them.

It is probably because of these competitive pressures that the networked data nightmare described in the NBC news report did not come to pass. Private enterprises soon realized that if they hoarded the collected data, they could use it as a moat against competitors, an advantage new entrants would be unable to match. And so, they actively resisted all efforts to network data, preferring to accumulate the data themselves to build a data monopoly. This resulted in our personal data being fragmented across all the various companies we patronized instead of being networked together in one single entity that anyone could access. In time, companies built large enough repositories of information about their customers to deliver insights that would otherwise not have been discernible. By slotting customers into categories – based on what they shopped for or the services they consumed – companies found that they could correlate exogenous data points to user profiles, accurately extrapolating behaviour across entire categories of customers.

As the data repositories grew, companies also realized that they could identify exactly what their customers wanted with increasing accuracy. This meant that they could target advertisements at them at precisely the moment when it was most likely to convert into a purchase. And so, they were able to nudge their customers to do their bidding.

Better than We Know Ourselves

A customer of a Target store outside Minneapolis walked in demanding to see the manager in something of a rage. Someone from the store had just sent his teenage daughter a bunch of shopping coupons for baby products and he was furious. 'She's still in high school,' he said, 'and you're sending her coupons for baby clothes and cribs? Are you trying to encourage her to get pregnant?' The poor store manager had no idea why she had been sent this material and could only assume that this was a mistake by the marketing department. So, he apologized as best he could, assuring the customer that this would not happen again. A couple of days later, the manager received a sheepish call from the irate customer who said he'd had a chat with his daughter, and she was, in fact, pregnant and due in a few months.

How did Target know that a young girl was pregnant before even her father did?

For years, Target had been assigning customers a unique 'Guest ID number' with which it associated the customer's purchases. This allowed them to amass customer data and helped them to target products more accurately. For instance, parents of little children could be sent catalogues of toys just in time for Christmas when they had the greatest likelihood of buying them. Those who bought swimsuits in April could be sent coupons for diet books in December.

The predictive analysis team at Target realized that, by far, the most effective way to change customers' shopping habits was by finding truly unique moments in their lives and focusing their marketing attention on that. If they could, at that precise moment, be targeted with suitable advertisements or coupons, Target could capture their spending as they began to spend in different ways. One such moment was pregnancy, a time when a mother was thinking about everything she had to do to prepare her family for the new child. If Target could determine which of their customers were pregnant and aim advertisements at them, they could capture that spend.

Soon, Target's predictive algorithm identified information related to over twenty-five product categories that allowed them to assign a 'pregnancy prediction' score to shoppers, narrowing their due date down to a small window. This included information as obscure as the fact that women, at the beginning of their second trimesters, tend to shift from scented to unscented lotions. Using these insights, they could time their coupons to reach prospective shoppers at precisely the right stage of their pregnancy to be most effective.

And that is how a large national supermarket chain knew more about the private life of a teenager in Minneapolis than her father did.

Data has always provided corporations powerful insights about their customers, allowing them to learn things about us that we do not fully appreciate. If Target could gather this level of intelligence from purchase data at their physical (offline) stores, imagine how much more powerful the insights that today's e-commerce stores can generate are.

Most of us make the vast majority of our purchases online. The platforms we use capture far more data about us than we realize. They know precisely what products we browsed through but did not buy, the time of the week and month we mostly make our purchases and the frequency with which we shop. They can correlate this information with a range of other factors to identify the products we are most likely to buy at a given point in time.

Recognizing the value of data, e-commerce sites do everything they can to collect as much data from us as is technically possible. Many of them use cross-app tracking technologies, embedding cookies into our browsers so that they can collect information about all the websites we visit. They associate all this information with our unique customer identity so that it can be funnelled back to the platform and processed, converting the breadcrumbs we leave behind in our browsing history into insights about our preferences and habits. This is why we often notice a spurt of advertisements related to the content of websites we visit soon after we have navigated away.

The opportunities that targeted advertising offers have forced companies to re-orient their operations to take advantage of them. This typically manifests in an increased volume of data collection – the more data, the better the insights.

Witness to a Crime

One way to take this data collection exercise even further is to gather information when the subject is away from their screen and keyboard. The ability to collect ambient data in unstructured environments when the subject is unaware that they may be contributing useful information can provide unexpected outcomes.

This is one of the reasons why we have seen an explosion of voice-enabled smart assistants capable of operating entirely through voice commands in a conversational interface. These are always at hand, listening to what we say to them and because of this, they extend the scope of data collection beyond the previously possible.

If the idea of having a device in our home that is always on, listening to everything we say sounds creepy, it doesn't seem to have affected the popularity of these devices. To many, the convenience of interacting with technology using a friendly voice interface is a trade-off they seem willing to make in exchange for giving up the personal information they make available in the process. Those who are marginally sceptical take comfort in manufacturers' assurances that these devices only turn themselves with a specific activation command and stay dormant at all other times.

But the moment you think about that assurance a bit more,

the more it becomes apparent how weak it is. In order for smart devices to wake up as soon as they are summoned they must, in fact, always be listening. They can't know we are calling unless they have one ear constantly open. We know this because we have all had moments when a random phrase uttered as part of a conversation has made a smart device switch on and start taking some action or the other. Who knows how many other times these devices might have turned themselves on in response to a misheard phrase and taken various autonomous measures on their own accord? Or what information they might have gathered about us without our knowledge?

When Victor Collins was discovered floating face-up in his friend's hot tub, the judge had no hesitation in issuing a search warrant for all 'audio recordings, transcribed records, text records, and other data' from the smart device in the house. The prosecution hoped that any recordings that might have been captured on that fateful night would offer insights into what had actually transpired during that night of drinking and watching football, and the judge did not see anything wrong in using the device to get to the truth. This begs the question of how safe we are in our own homes when our smart assistants turn informers for the police.

In another incident, this time involving domestic violence, a smart device that had turned itself on during a heated (and violent) argument misheard the angry boyfriend's repeated screams at his girlfriend: 'Did you call the sheriff? Did you call the sheriff?' as an instruction and phoned the sheriff's department of its own accord. To their credit, the companies involved have always resisted the request to turn over information, usually only acquiescing when they get an order from the court. But how long before providing access to the data becomes the norm?

But that is not the only category of smart device that can provide useful evidence about us to law enforcement. When sixty-seven-year-old Karen Navarra was murdered in her house in San Jose, California, on 13 September 2018, the police were puzzled. Her stepfather, Anthony Aiello, had briefly visited that afternoon to drop off some homemade pizza and biscotti, and he confirmed that his stepdaughter was alive when he had left. But as the investigation wore on, the police discovered from the Fitbit fitness tracker Karen was wearing that her heart rate had spiked significantly around 3.20 p.m. when she was still with Aiello in her apartment and that it slowed down rapidly to a halt at 3.28 p.m., a full five minutes before the neighbours confirmed he left. This was enough for Anthony to be arrested for her murder.

The devices we wear offer inadvertent insights into our behaviour. There was a time when Fitbits recorded users' sexual activity and, thanks to what I can only assume to be an accidental error, made it possible for this information to be published online. Since most users had their activity logs set to public access by default, all their friends got to see whether they were engaged in 'mild to moderate', 'passive, light effort', or 'active and vigorous' sexual activity.

When Strava (a website designed to offer deep insights into athletic performance) released a global heat map of where people exercise, it disclosed, without realizing it, classified information about the deployment of American troops in potentially sensitive military sites in Afghanistan and Syria. It also geolocated the secret headquarters of Taiwan's missile command that housed the defensive long-range weapons it had trained on China.

There is little doubt that the technology we surround ourselves with – the websites we visit, the applications we use, the smart machines around us – know more about us than we do ourselves. We trust that the companies who control them will use this knowledge for the purposes they say they will and nothing more. But this is blind faith. The companies' actions are impossible to verify because they take place behind a veil. The algorithms of these websites and the technologies packed into the electronics around us are so complex, so intricately interwoven with other systems, that it is impossible for anyone, including the companies that run them, to fully understand everything they are capable of and what they actually do.

What we do know for certain is that none of us have anything close to the level of autonomy we believe we do over our digital lives. Even when we think we control the decisions we make – what we buy, the places we eat at or where we decide to go for a vacation – our path has, at least to some extent, been influenced by the electronic companions we keep.

Electronic Influence

In 2018, British political consulting firm, Cambridge Analytica, was accused of collecting the personal data of millions of Facebook users and using it to target potential voters with personalized ads during the US presidential election and the UK Brexit Referendum, both of which took place in 2016. The company used the data it had collected from Facebook users to build psychological profiles about them, based on which they would target voters with advertising designed to appeal to their emotions and prejudices. By identifying small, persuadable groups, it was possible to target micro-advertising at them in ways guaranteed to change their minds.

For instance, Cambridge Analytica discovered a strong correlation between individuals who owned American-made products (Ford vehicles and the like) and registered Republicans. They used this insight to target patriotic content at Ford car owners who were not Republican voters in the hope that by inundating them with all-American ads, voters on the fence might be nudged more firmly into the Republican camp. Similar tactics were used in the UK during the Brexit vote as Cambridge Analytica worked with the Leave Campaign to target voters with advertisements designed to stoke their fears of immigrants and the European Union.

This is just one example (albeit the most egregious and publicly visible) of how the digital insights collected about us can be insidiously used to achieve hidden objectives. Secret insights about our hidden beliefs and desires can be used to manipulate how we think about a candidate or vote in a referendum.

How did we allow this to happen?

It is no secret that most internet businesses earn revenue not from the customers to whom they most directly provide their services but from the advertisers who use their sites to target customers. As a result, their ability to grow their revenue does not depend as much on the services they offer as on their ability to accurately target advertisements to those most likely to buy them. If the services they provide make us want to continue to use their products, it has less to do with them wanting to keep us happy than it does with the fact that retaining us as captive customers improves their odds of improving the accuracy of their targeted advertising. Given that their entire business model is based on advertising revenue, it is little wonder that the minor inconveniences that this causes are rarely a cause for concern.

Take the case of Heidi Waterhouse, who, after traumatically losing a much-wanted pregnancy, kept seeing advertisements for products for a newborn even after manually unsubscribing herself from every email provider she could think of. Or Carly-May Kavanagh, whose polycystic ovary syndrome made it incredibly difficult, if not impossible, to conceive, but who still kept getting sent advertisements for maternity clothes and baby toys on her social feeds.

Ask anyone who gambles online, and they will tell you how advertisements for short-term loan products miraculously appear just as they are running short of the funds needed to keep their winning streak going or the pressures that those struggling with alcohol addiction face when shown advertisements of the very products they are trying so desperately to avoid.

These advertisements are not mistakes. They are, on the contrary, evidence of how well the algorithm is working. When recovering alcoholics are shown liquor advertisements, they see it precisely because the algorithm knows how much they want it and how likely it is that they can be enticed into purchasing it. Among those most likely to buy alcohol, recently recovering alcoholics must be high on the list.

Tone Deaf and Colour Blind

One of the reasons why we began to use algorithms in the first place was because we know that human decision-makers are weak. Their decisions are often coloured by personal impressions and circumstances, sometimes even the time of day. We thought we needed to take them out of the equation so that the decisions affecting the lives of ordinary people were not subject to the vagaries of human bias. Thus, we turned to algorithms, trusting that they would take the capriciousness out of decision-making and, if we could provide them with all the relevant facts, they would dispassionately arrive at a fair decision.

In hindsight, having now used algorithms like these for a few decades, we know that, while they may not have all the same blind spots as humans, they are not as unbiased as we had hoped. Based as they are on data generated by human processes, algorithms reflect the same flaws and failings as the humans they learnt from.

Around 2010, when the Los Angeles Police Department carried out an algorithmic analysis of the more than 13 million crimes that had occurred in the city in an eight-decade period, they noticed trends in the data that were mathematically congruent with the equations that predict the aftershocks of an earthquake. This allowed them to calculate where crimes were likely to occur on a given day so that they could deploy patrols in those neighbourhoods preventively. Thus was borne the concept of predictive policing.

In short order, cities around the US and countries around the world began to deploy these measures to optimize the efficiency of their police forces, which were never going to be large enough to cover every neighbourhood in their cities. What they were doing was straight out of *The Minority Report*, a real-world precognition approach that was surprisingly effective. Until it wasn't.

As we discovered much later, in addition to identifying patterns in the live data, PredPol was overlaying statistical information drawn from historical data sets to improve the accuracy of the results. This meant that neighbourhoods historically prone to crime tended to be the target of police attention – even if their residents were doing nothing wrong. But because the police were always there on patrol, even the most minor transgressions were caught and punished, dooming certain localities to a never-ending downward spiral from which they could not escape.

If law enforcement must be fair and impartial, the judiciary must be even more so. Judges rule on whether those who come before them are guilty or not and, if they are, what punishments they must suffer. Since, in many cases, these punishments could extend to incarceration and worse, they need to be extra careful about leaving their personal biases at the door – both about the culpability of the individual concerned as well as the extent of punishment they should bear.

Recidivism risk is the likelihood that a convict will repeat the offence he was incarcerated for once released from prison. Before pronouncing a sentence, judges need to assess the recidivism risk of the accused to ensure that the punishment they mete out is sufficient to significantly reduce the likelihood of a repeat offence. But even though they must objectively assess the risk on several different parameters, judges are as human as the rest of us. Try as they might, their biases shape their perspective, and time and again, this has affected the sentences they have handed down.

For instance, judges with daughters are more likely to rule favourably towards women compared to their colleagues who do not. Similarly, there is evidence to suggest that judges are more likely to award bail if they have just come back from a recess, compared to those approaching a food break. In a study in the United Kingdom, eighty-one judges were presented with various hypothetical situations and asked to decide whether they would award bail to the imaginary defendants, they failed to agree on a single one of the forty-one cases presented to them.

This is not good news for any legal system because it is supposed to provide certainty to those being judged. If anything, it proves that no sentence handed down by a human judge is likely to be objective. When the likelihood of conviction has a more significant correlation to the time of day and the workload of the court than to the merits of the case being argued, we must do something to fix our justice system.

In an attempt to address some of these human frailties, courts in the US began to using algorithms for sentencing. Having determined the guilt of the accused, they decided to design an algorithm to assess the recidivism risk based on all the relevant factors. Since the algorithm was not subject to any biases that humans find surprisingly hard to ignore, they believed these determinations would be fair and impartial.

As it happens, they were not.

In 2013, when Paul Zilly was convicted of stealing a lawnmower in Wisconsin, he agreed to a plea deal because both the prosecution and the defence concurred that the circumstances of his crime did not warrant a lengthy jail term. Before he confirmed the plea deal, the judge ran the case through a sentencing algorithm to make sure that setting him free would not have any negative consequences. The algorithm suggested that Zilly, a black man, posed a high risk for violent crime. Faced with this analysis, the judge felt obliged to reject the plea deal even though the prosecutor had agreed that there was no need to send Zilly to jail.

Assessing recidivism risk involves analysing pertinent factors related to a convicted person in order to evaluate the likelihood of their return to a life of crime after they have been released from jail. While the algorithm might be impartial, historical biases in the law enforcement system tend to punish some categories of people more harshly than others. If a poorer locality has historically had higher levels of crime than more affluent ones, residents of those areas are likely to be adjudged by the algorithm as posing a higher recidivism risk. Similar prejudices have resulted in people of colour being convicted of an offence even though that individual doesn't pose a greater risk than a white one. While these algorithms might have eliminated or moderated the effect of human biases at the individual level, they have still allowed historical biases perpetuated against entire classes of society to persist.

Biases find their way into algorithms in all manner of different ways. During the COVID-19 pandemic, when we were forced to use contactless technologies, the racism inherent in everyday technologies became painfully apparent. In the US, while most automatic hand sanitizers and soap dispensers had no problem recognizing the Caucasian hands being waved beneath them, they struggled to respond to hands of darker complexions. In a far more distressing incident, a photo storage site automatically tagged images of African Americans as gorillas even though it had no trouble accurately identifying those of paler complexions as people.

Generative AI – which is all the rage now – is surprisingly

prone to gender bias. When I first got a Midjourney subscription, I tried to get the AI image generator to create images of doctors, lawyers and every other category of professional that I could think of. Almost without exception, each of the image sets it generated were almost entirely male, as if in the AI world, there were no women doctors, lawyers or entrepreneurs. When I ran a prompt to generate images of models, dancers and homemakers, the images were overwhelmingly female.

Similar studies have been carried out in relation to occupational biases in other generative language models. These models were found to make occupational associations for different categories of persons based on gender, religion, sexuality, ethnicity, political affiliation and continental name origin. For example, in general, machine-predicted jobs tend to be less diverse and more stereotypical for women than for men, reflecting, for the most part, the skewed gender and ethnic distribution in existing societal biases.

We convinced ourselves that the machines we introduced into our decision-making processes were impartial and emotionless, their decisions the outcome of cold, hard logic incapable of being influenced by feelings and historical prejudice. So, we ignored the machine-driven outcomes that seemed unfair, preferring to trust the machine over the evidence of our eyes. We supressed our niggling doubts over these decisions, convincing ourselves that the machine must know facts that were not immediately evident to their human operators, that their mechanical precision made it impossible for them to generate biased outcomes.

Until the evidence was too overwhelming to ignore.

It is hard to judge which is worse: allowing humans to make decisions about other humans, knowing that the prejudices that

drive them will inevitably lead to injustice, or allowing a machine
to take those decisions based solely on the emotionless logic
of an algorithm, when the mathematical decision tree of the
algorithm has imbibed the prejudices embedded in the historical
data from which it was derived.

Data Regulation

'The Internet is the first thing that humanity has built that humanity doesn't understand, the largest experiment in anarchy that we have ever had.'

– Eric Schmidt

If we were to sum up the concerns around data and data technologies, they would boil down to three issues: the surveillance risk they pose, the extent to which these technologies could be used to invade our privacy and the harm that we could face because of automated decision-making.

In the hands of an authoritarian or illiberal government, data technologies can be used to identify individuals in a crowd, to track their whereabouts and monitor their activities for political ends. Irresponsible corporations could use them to track behavioural patterns to target purchases at potential customers when they are most likely to succumb to the temptation. In the process, these technologies impinge upon our privacy in ways that were unimaginable even a decade ago.

By accumulating data in easily searchable databases, they can be processed, categorized and analysed to enable those controlling the data to know us in ways that no stranger could. When combined with technologies capable of observing us – cameras, wearable devices, smart assistants and even our mobile phones – we can find ourselves subject to a level of surveillance in our daily lives that, at this scale, is unprecedented in human history. When we experimented with something like this in incarceration facilities, we found that constant surveillance can be tremendously harmful to the psyche. And yet the world we live in has been designed to do just that – expose every facet of our daily lives and subject us to such constant scrutiny that it must have some impact on our psychological development.

The insights these data systems generate are built by invading our privacy and unearthing aspects of ourselves that we have kept secret, even from those closest to us. They use this information to erode our autonomy – they provide us recommendations for what we should do next and, in the process, limit the full range of choices we might have made. We have grown so accustomed to relying on these algorithms for suggestions that we are unaware of how they shape what we are exposed to. Any decision we think we are making has, to a large extent, already been made for us.

Few appreciate the extent to which the decisions of these machines are influenced by the human biases and prejudices inherent in the data sets on which they are trained. Even though the answers they provide may be the answers we need, they have been arrived at based on past decisions and incorporate the *same* human flaws the machines were brought in to avoid.

While this may not make much of a difference when all we want is a suggestion for what book to read or what movie to watch next, when algorithms are used to decide questions like what bail should be set for a crime or what sentence should be imposed, bias of any sort is a concern.

Any of these three concerns – surveillance, privacy and bias – should be a cause for alarm, prompting nations globally to take action to mitigate them and protect their citizens from the consequences. To achieve this, regulations could be enacted to ensure that users modify their behaviour to mitigate potential risks.

To be fair, this is hard to do. Technology regulation calls for weighing all potential benefits against unavoidable harms, a calculus nearly impossible to do during the early stages of the evolution of a technology when it may have a tangible benefit. This is further complicated by how hard it is to appreciate the full potential of new technology without allowing it to grow without restraint. It is only when technology grows and evolves in unpredictable directions that the possibilities of what it could do to and for us are revealed. Yet, there is no doubt that appropriate constraints are necessary to ensure that serious harms do not ensue.

This is why most technology regulations have been largely ineffective. They either err too much on the side of nurturing private innovation, providing companies with such strong protections against liability that they have no incentive to do what is necessary to mitigate ancillary harms. Or, they end up overcompensating for the harms that these technologies may cause, imposing so many restraints on their functioning that they end up stifling innovation.

We need to navigate a path between these two extremes, to try and find a way to impose just enough restraint on technology so that the companies deploying it don't run amok, but not so much that the effort of complying with the law ends up being so onerous that companies crumble under the weight of regulation.

But to figure out this middle ground, we need to understand how we got here in the first place.

The History of Data Regulation

For most of its early history, the internet was not regulated. Few understood what it was about or how it worked. As a result, regulators left well alone, allowing the ecosystem to flourish, unencumbered by compliance obligations.

This hands-off approach came under pressure when the internet evolved to allow users to generate content themselves. With more and more people posting whatever they wanted online, what some users thought was acceptable was viewed by others as offensive and potentially illegal. Since those who uploaded content were either anonymous or unverifiable, website owners were held liable for the content on their sites instead.

Had things carried on this way, it would have been the end of the nascent internet. Platform owners who found themselves liable for what users said and did online would have shut down their websites, unwilling – and in most cases unable – to take responsibility for the irresponsible actions of those who visited their sites. If they were to carry on doing what they were doing, they needed protection from liability for the acts of strangers that they did not control. Unless the question of liability was framed differently, the internet, as it existed then, was doomed to fail before it had even begun.

One of the ways in which early internet businesses attempted to absolve themselves of liability was by suggesting that, just as the distributors of books and magazines cannot be liable for the content contained in them, the owner of a website should not be held responsible for what users post online. Distributors of magazines simply stock what they receive in their stores. If it happens that the content of any of those magazines is illegal, there is not a lot they can do to change it. Publishers, on the other hand, have much more control over what appears in the pages of their magazines. Since they retain ultimate editorial control over what is finally printed, publishers cannot point to the author and absolve themselves of liability if the content they publish causes harm.

The immunity of booksellers from liability for the content of the books they sell had already been established in 1959 in *Smith v. California*, a case in which the US Supreme Court ruled that holding booksellers liable for obscene materials in their stores violated the right to freedom of speech. The court went on to underscore the chilling effect that this sort of standard could have on the dissemination of constitutionally protected material.

The principle set out in *Smith* was later extended to the internet in 1991 in *Cubby, Inc. v. CompuServe Inc.*. This case involved CompuServe, an online service provider, that was sought to be held liable for defamatory content posted by a third party on one of its forums. The plaintiff argued that CompuServe had control over the content on its platform and should not, as a result, be entitled to the protection extended to distributors. Since it was a distributor of information, it was responsible for ensuring that defamatory content was not published on the platform. The court disagreed on the grounds that the company had no knowledge of the content and did not exercise editorial control over the forum in which it was posted. CompuServe, it held, was a passive distributor of information and accordingly entitled to protection from liability.

This issue was tested one more time in *Stratton Oakmont, Inc. v. Prodigy Services Co.*, where, in 1995, the New York Supreme Court was called upon to determine whether Prodigy, an online service provider, should be held liable for defamatory statements made by an anonymous user on its platform. The plaintiff argued that, unlike CompuServ, Prodigy actively moderated and controlled the content on its platform. Since it was an active moderator and in control of the information that was posted, its operations were more akin to a publisher than a passive distributor of information. The court agreed and ruled: 'It is Prodigy's own policies, technology and staffing decisions which have altered the scenario and mandated the finding that it is a publisher.' It held the company liable for the content on its site precisely because it was committed to removing unwholesome content.

Good Samaritans

Two young US senators – Ron Wyden (a Republican from California) and Chris Cox (a Democrat from Oregon) – thought the decision in *Stratton Oakmont v. Prodigy* was perverse. Prodigy was trying to make the internet better by moderating the content on its site and taking down objectionable content posted by third parties so that other users could have a better experience. But it is precisely because they were being Good Samaritans, cleaning up after those who had irresponsibly made a mess that they were now being punished by being reclassified as publishers and denied the protection that CompuServ had received. According to Wyden and Cox, not only was this ruling absurd, but it would sound the death knell for a promising new industry sorely in need of nurturing. What was required was a law that would protect websites from the liability that arose precisely because they were being good citizens and making the internet a better place for everyone else.

The senators set out to right that wrong by enacting a law that would overturn the precedent set by *Stratton Oakmont v. Prodigy*, and in the process, they influenced how countries around the world came to think about content liability. They introduced a new section, Section 230, into the Communications Decency Act, 1996, effectively offering online platforms immunity from liability for user-generated content:

The operative part of the section is just twenty-six words, so I am going to reproduce it here in its entirety:

'No provider or user of an interactive computer service shall be treated as the publisher or speaker of any information provided by another information content provider.'

In these twenty-six short words, Section 230 established a legal framework that sheltered internet businesses from liability for user-generated content. It ensured that they no longer had to worry about trying to design their business to look like distributors and not publishers but instead gave them free rein to innovate as they chose, secure in the assurance that they would not be held responsible for how users chose to use their service.

Section 230 sent a strong signal to the courts that the fledgling internet industry had to be protected. The courts responded by swinging the pendulum so far in the opposite direction that the series of cases that followed its enactment assured internet companies of such a broad legal shield against prosecution that they had very little incentive to monitor the content uploaded to their sites. This resulted in the unchecked proliferation of hate speech, harassment and misinformation online, the consequences of which we are dealing with to this day.

Internet Exceptionalism

The enactment of Section 230 and the judicial decisions that subsequently elevated it to its current importance gave rise to the concept of internet exceptionalism – the notion that online businesses were fundamentally different from traditional brick-and-mortar operations – and must, therefore, be held to a different standard. That the laws and regulations that apply to the rest of the world must work differently in the online context. Once established, this idea took root and extended far beyond online content regulation.

In the context of competition, for instance, internet platforms have argued that network effects offer benefits to customers and that consolidating internet businesses into massive monolithic platforms is not the problem antitrust law would have you believe. If there was just one big platform that serves all a user's needs, they no longer need to go from portal to portal to find what they want. Thanks to the zero marginal cost of distribution in the online context, what might have been a monopoly in the brick-and-mortar world was a consumer benefit. They also argue that this is good for sellers who can similarly take advantage of the large marketplace of potential buyers instead of listing their goods and services on multiple apps.

Similar arguments have been raised in the context of the borderless nature of online services. Since the internet can be accessed from anywhere, no single country should be able to assert tax jurisdiction over online transactions since this would result in all jurisdictions asserting such claims over them. This, they argue, could destroy the viability of the online business model that we have all come to rely upon.

But internet exceptionalism has another, altogether more insidious consequence. When it becomes the norm for certain businesses to get exemptions from existing laws, they tend to be left alone, unconstrained by the regulations and compliances that other companies have to contend with. In the process, they are accountable to no one but themselves for the ways in which their business models are designed, the relationship they build with their customers and the liberties they can take with them. Almost from the very beginning, internet businesses have danced to their own tune, operating according to a set of terms and conditions they set for themselves.

And over which few have a say.

Surveillance Capitalism

From this lack of regulation and freedom from restraint grew the business models and data practices that have come to characterize the modern data economy. As we have seen, data is collected from us wherever we go. It is collected by third parties we know – the local grocery store whose loyalty programme we are part of and the gym that keeps track of our workout routine and our meal plans – as well as those we don't. We allow the devices we wear to access information about where we go, how long we walk and what we photograph. We allow the devices around us, in our homes and offices, to remember what we search for and discern our current mood from the type of music we listen to. Anyone who loves gadgets (like I do) is bleeding data every minute of every day.

This data is put to work to identify us. To slot us into buckets, placing us into categories based on whatever purpose the companies collecting this data want to achieve. The more categories we can be slotted into, the better it is because it is by understanding how these different categories intersect that the machine learns how to create narrower, more finely grained profiles of who we are and what drives us. And when they have managed to slot us into all these buckets, nameless, faceless entities that we have never met will end up knowing us better than we do ourselves.

In almost every instance, these insights are used for commercial advantage. To direct advertising at us with such fine-grained accuracy that it reaches us at the precise moment we are most likely to buy whatever the advertiser is selling. To evaluate whether we are worthy of the services we might have applied for – a loan, a job, or insurance for our car – and to monitor whether we will continue to be so throughout that service.

It has, as a result, assumed tremendous commercial significance, giving rise to what Shoshana Zuboff calls surveillance capitalism, a new form of capitalism that incentivizes technology companies to collect, analyse and profit from personal data. Unlike traditional capitalism, where businesses extract value from the production and exchange of goods and services, in surveillance capitalism, value is created through the monitoring, analysis and manipulation of human behaviour.

Zuboff believes that surveillance capitalism is the commodification of personal data by creating 'behavioural surplus.' This allows businesses to build 'prediction products' that are then sold to willing buyers who use them to influence behaviour and manipulate consumer choices. This means that companies can shift focus from meeting the existing needs of their customers to predicting what their needs might be and shaping their behaviours to nudge them in the direction of these potential needs they could fulfil. Not only does this impact individual autonomy and privacy, it also gives businesses the incentive to subject their customers to constant monitoring, manipulation and commodification.

The Attention Economy and Filter Bubbles

If behavioural surplus is a valuable commodity, companies must find ways to generate more of it. They need to keep users on their site for as long as possible so that through their interactions with the content on it, they can improve their insights of them.

To do this, they have to design offerings to hold customers' attention for the greatest possible duration. And they have to do it better than the competition. Tristan Harris argues that this is why we are currently living in an attention economy, where technology companies are fighting each other for a share of our attention. One way in which this manifests is through the technology designed to keep users engaged and scrolling for as long as possible. This is achieved through a series of software choices – infinite scrolling, push notifications and personalized content recommendations, all of which are designed to ensure that users voluntarily spend more time on the platform.

These seemingly innocuous design choices have significant consequences for society. When algorithms are designed to curate and present personalized content to users, they study their past behaviour, interests and preferences and use the insights accumulated over scores of past user interactions to determine the next piece of content that will be relevant and interesting to the user. They present each new item and measure the user's response to evaluate whether they liked it or not so that they can use that understanding to refine their recommendations further. When applied to content for entertainment, this results in a steady stream of music of a given genre or movies of a particular type. When applied to news or opinions, it creates a self-reinforcing cycle of confirmation bias, in which individuals only get to see content that reinforces their pre-existing beliefs and perspectives.

This is what Eli Parser refers to as a filter bubble, the phenomenon where internet users become isolated in their informational cocoon and where all they see is content aligning with their existing beliefs and preferences. As a result, they get increasingly detached from reality, to the point where they refuse to entertain positions divergent from their own. Filter bubbles make it harder for individuals to encounter new ideas and perspectives. This, in turn, contributes to the spread of misinformation and fake news, leading to the spread of conspiracy theories and other forms of alternate facts that can significantly impact public opinion and political discourse.

The consequence of filter bubbles is the extreme political polarization of society – to the point where different factions exist in their echo chambers, incapable of reaching across the aisle to shake the hand of a neighbour from another camp.

They become entrenched in their views, refusing to engage in productive debate with anyone who holds a different perspective, and this leads to a gridlock that will inevitably lead to the decline of society.

Today, data is both the raw material and the means of production of the modern economy. It is often used in ways that are not in the interests of those it pertains to. It is put to uses that far exceed the purposes for which it was collected and retained longer than required because no one knows when it might be useful. Even though data fiduciaries assure us that they will only collect as much data as is *strictly necessary* for them to achieve their stated purpose, they end up collecting *as much as they possibly can* so that they never want for data when required and are free to derive as much information and as many insights from it as possible.

The businesses that control the spigot of the data firehose are, today, among the most valuable on the planet. They have more customers than the population of large countries and their most minor decisions affect the lives and livelihoods of billions. They are among the most powerful entities on the planet, with the ability to control what we get to see and what we don't. And as a result, they can influence our beliefs, shape our decisions and change our minds.

Govern Thyself

When Senators Wyden and Cox introduced Section 230 into the Communications Decency Act, 1996, they believed that instead of trying to find offline equivalents for online activities – as the courts had been doing till that point – what was needed was a new framework to govern the online world. Judging by the explosion of innovation that followed, their intervention was successful.

But instead of coming up with that new legal framework, they simply created an exception from liability and left it to the companies to figure out how to regulate the activities of their users. In hindsight, that was perhaps unwise. By giving rise to the notion of internet exceptionalism, tech companies came to believe they were fundamentally different from their offline counterparts, entitled to be held to a completely new set of legal standards. By allowing companies to determine how online spaces should be governed, our interactions came to be judged, not in relation to national laws and regulations, but to the terms of service and privacy policies of the platforms they controlled.

As a result, we no longer have a reasonable expectation of privacy in our online interactions. The platforms we use are constantly watching us, tuning their algorithms to deeply personalize their engagement with us. The data they collect is processed in ways we can never fully appreciate and used to profile us into categories we never knew we fitted into. We are fed content that algorithms believe we want to see and grouped with others who think like us in ever narrower and more finely defined ways.

All of this has led to unprecedented levels of polarization in society, to a social fragmentation that has altered the course of national elections and made enemies of lifelong friends. It has destroyed trust in institutions and the truth, encouraging tribal groups to coalesce around their own version of what is real in ways that make the gaps between them impossible to bridge.

While the laissez-faire approach to data regulation that developed as a natural consequence of the original Cox and Wyden legislation was perhaps necessary to help the internet survive in its initial years, it is now abundantly clear that leaving data businesses to regulate themselves is not a winning strategy. And if the US would not do anything about it, legislators across the pond were more than willing to step in to fill the breach.

Meanwhile in Europe . . .

Since more global technology businesses are based in the US than anywhere else, the economic benefits of the data industry accrue most directly to that country. As a result, the US has the greatest incentive to ensure that the regulatory burden on internet companies is as light as possible.

Other countries, usually the consumers of all that US tech giants have to offer, tend to be much less sanguine about this approach. Since the value generated from this data tends to accrue to the US registered companies that collect it, they see little benefit in allowing such data collection to continue unchecked. What's more, when evidence surfaced of how this data was being used to cause harm to their people, they had every incentive to crack down on these practices to mitigate this risk. This is why most countries outside the US rarely allow market forces to act so freely, choosing instead to enact a range of different types of regulations to rein data businesses in.

Europe probably has the most stringent data regulations in the world. Its data protection law, the General Data Protection Regulation (GDPR), is widely recognized as the gold standard that other countries must aspire to. Based on this legislation,

European data regulators have repeatedly found the US approach to data protection 'inadequate', putting critical cross-border data flows at risk between the two continents.

In addition, European competition regulators have their sights firmly trained on US tech companies, regularly imposing significant fines on their operations, arguing that they are fundamentally anti-competitive and that their mergers and acquisitions strategies are designed to create dominant enterprises that violates EU competition law. As an approach, this is almost diametrically the opposite of the US model. Instead of allowing market forces to determine behaviour, it lists, in excruciating detail, precisely what each data business needs to do when dealing with data, requiring them to put in place a large organization just to deal with compliance.

It is, for all intents and purposes, the dominant approach to data regulation worldwide, and it is worth examining in some more detail exactly how Europe's data regulations have been designed to function.

Data Protection in Europe

Europe has a characteristically citizen-centric approach to data protection. It is hard to say whether this is a reaction to what the continent endured during the Second World War or simply due to the high premium they place on human rights. Regardless, from the very early days of the computer revolution, businesses in Europe have faced a higher compliance burden than anywhere else in the world.

As data businesses began to flourish and grow, Europe enacted a series of legislative measures curb their activities. These regulations focused mostly on the harms that ordinary citizens could suffer if they engaged with these new data businesses. It began in 1981 when the Council of Europe enacted the Convention for the Protection of Individuals with regard to Automatic Processing of Personal Data. They established several key principles that became a core part of data protection regulations globally. Most significantly, they made consent central to the governance framework, obliging data fiduciaries to obtain informed consent from the data principal before collecting and processing data.

At around the same time, the need was felt to elevate data protection to a fundamental human right. Thus, privacy and data protection concepts were included in the Universal Declaration of Human Rights, which resulted in a rich human rights jurisprudence being developed around the subject. This was eventually codified into the European Union's (EU) Data Protection Directive of 1995, which established for the first time a regulatory framework for protecting personal data within the EU.

In 2016, the EU upgraded the Directive into the GDPR, a full-blown regulation which, when it came into effect in 2018, became the most advanced data protection framework in the world. It represented an approach to data governance that was almost the polar opposite of the US's, imposing strict compliance obligations on data businesses by curtailing how much data they could collect and the uses to which it could be put. They believed this would give data principals more direct control over what is done with their personal data, both what was collected and how it was used.

Data Protection Principles

Data protection law has a rich jurisprudence of case law and subordinate regulation. Getting into those nuances is beyond the scope of this book, but if I were to summarize the governance framework that the GDPR describes, it is aligned around a set of privacy principles that limit what can be done with personal data and outlines the rights that data principals have. These principles can be broadly categorized as falling within one or more of the following:

- those that ensure users' autonomy over their data;
- those that protect against disproportionate access; and
- those that require confidentiality and security of the data

Autonomy, in the context of personal data, is the ability to determine what can or cannot be done with it. While there are many ways in which this can be implemented, the foremost among these is through the mechanism of consent, which is why it lies at the heart of most data protection legislations and forms the cornerstone of the privacy strategy of most data businesses.

Consent is typically useful when data is collected, serving as the primary ground under which that data can be processed. However, most data protection laws also offer other rights that data principals can invoke to exercise their autonomy over their personal data. For instance, data principals have the right to require data fiduciaries to confirm whether they are processing any personal data about that data principal and, if so, they can demand access to this information. They also have the right to correct any personal information that is found to be inaccurate or require information that has served its purpose to be deleted.

European data protection laws also extend the principle of personal autonomy to personal data of the data principal that is under the control of the data fiduciary. Data principals have a right to data portability, which is the ability to insist that any data fiduciary holding their data must, on request, transfer that data either to the data principals themselves or to any other data fiduciary the data principal designates as a recipient.

Once collected, the data moves into the hands of the data fiduciary. To prevent them from misusing the data entrusted into their care, European regulations impose constraints on what can be done with it. These provisions, designed to protect against indiscriminate access and use, operate regardless of any consent that the data fiduciary might have obtained to the contrary.

At the most basic level, this is spelled out in the regulation in the form of purpose limitation provisions that stipulate that data fiduciaries can only collect data for specific, clearly specified purposes. This means that no data principal can be asked to agree to a purpose that is too broadly defined or unnecessarily general. Data fiduciaries are also obliged to adhere to data minimization obligations which require them to collect only as much data as is strictly necessary to fulfil their stated purposes – and no more. This suggests that, even if the data fiduciary has been permitted to collect data for a specified purpose, it must collect no more data than absolutely necessary to achieve that purpose.

Similar stipulations also exist in relation to the retention of data after its immediate purpose is served. Unless expressly stipulated in the privacy policy, data cannot be retained for longer than required to fulfil its purpose, after which it must be deleted. Finally, all data protection regulations have use-limitation obligations that stipulate that data fiduciaries can only use data for the precise purposes for which it was collected and nothing else.

Since all the data in question is personal – and often sensitive – there is a need to ensure that it remains confidential and secure. The data fiduciary functions as a custodian of the data collected from data principals and is obliged, for as long as that data remains within its care, to ensure its security and integrity. This extends to making sure that data is secure against not only a potential data breach or cyberattack but also phishing and other attempts to use social engineering and physical breach of data storage systems. When such data is transferred to a third party for processing, the data fiduciary must still ensure the confidentiality of that data.

Is This Still Relevant?

These data protection principles, in some shape or form, have been in use for three decades now and are almost universally recognized as the necessary compliance standards for adequate personal data protection. However, more recently, questions have been raised about their continued effectiveness.

Take consent, for example. In most instances, it is a necessary prerequisite to availing a service, and data principals have no option but to provide consent when it is asked for in relation to a service they cannot do without. Since getting consent is so cumbersome, data fiduciaries prefer to obtain, upfront, consent for as many potential uses as possible. As a result, it is often requested in such broad terms that it typically extends to various potential uses beyond its immediate purpose.

We are bombarded by an ever-expanding number of consent

requests, resulting in consent fatigue that makes us loathe to even attempt to apply our minds to each new data request. As a result, no one actually reads the terms and clicks 'I Accept' without any further thought to the consequences. This is either blind trust – the belief that modern data businesses will not do anything that violates the trust that their customers have reposed in them – or it is because we have intuitively realized that there is no way we can ever fully appreciate what it means to consent to the things data companies require us to.

There is a paradox inherent in consent that makes it pointless to rely on it for data protection. For consent to be truly *informed*, we need to be provided with enough information about the data collected from us to make a calculated decision – what it is going to be used for, how long it will be retained, whom it will be shared with and for what purpose will it be used. If we are not given that granular level of information, the consent we provide cannot truly be *informed*. And yet, if we were given that information for every piece of data collected from us, the number of different considerations we would need to process to accurately assess the ways in which our privacy could be affected would be so mind-bogglingly complex that it would be impossible for us to evaluate meaningfully.

For our decisions to be truly informed, we need more data than our privacy policies currently contain. But if they contain all the information we need for our decision to be truly informed, it would be too complex for us to understand.

Even if we do find a solution to these problems, modern data practices will defeat all attempts at rational assessment. Today, data sets are layered in ways that make the data within them impossible to classify. Information that was not personal when collected could, when placed in conjunction with information accumulated through these layered data sets, generate insights that are, in fact, deeply personal. What was anonymous when collected could, as more data is added, begin to be deanonymized and reidentify you to the point where the consent we provided yesterday will be meaningless tomorrow.

If consent is largely meaningless in the modern context, the principles of purpose limitation and retention restriction are easily evaded obligations. Given how difficult it is to keep collecting consent from data principals, most data businesses stipulate (despite the prohibition against overly broad specifications) the purposes for which they collect data in such generic terms that the widest possible range of data would qualify for collection. When the purpose has been specified like this, it justifies retention for far longer than would otherwise have been necessary. Purpose limitations and retention restrictions were included in the statute to constrain the amount of data collected and the uses to which it could be put. But modern data businesses have learnt to work their way around these restrictions to not only have as much data as they need but retain it for as long as necessary.

Similar challenges apply to use limitation restrictions. For these stipulations to work, they need to operate as an effective constraint on using the data for anything other than the specified purposes. This is, as one can imagine, hard to police. Once data has been legitimately collected, it passes into the control of the data fiduciary, at which point it becomes virtually impossible to identify what is done with it. It is, therefore, practically impossible to enforce the use limitation obligation in a meaningful way to ensure absolute compliance with its provisions with any degree of certainty. At best, violations can be detected after the fact – when evidence of the resultant harm from such transgressions surfaces. This typically happens long after the misuse has taken place and it is not a particularly effective measure to mitigate harm.

Finally, as much as one might think that the right to data portability offers data principals genuine autonomy and control over their data – because they can use it to access information controlled by data fiduciaries – this is a right that is very hard to enforce in a way that really benefits the data principal. Since data portability is a standard requirement under most modern data protection regulations, data fiduciaries around the world have taken steps to put in place measures that give effect to it. On request, most of them will make this data available to the data principal, but they will do so in one giant data dump that fulfils the letter, not the spirit, of the law. Getting this sort of unprocessed history of our interactions serves no greater purpose than as an offline backup should we require it. The effort of finding any useful information from this data is often beyond the capability of the average person.

The Problem with Regulation

The data protection principles that form the basis of Europe's data protection regulations were written for a simpler time, when data was collected for narrow and identifiable uses which made evaluating the consequences of providing consent relatively trivial. Once it became easy to store data and access it on the fly from vast cloud computing resources for analysis, these principles began to come under stress.

Today, there is increasing consensus that the European

approach to data protection is not working as was originally intended. The restrictions it imposes on what can be done with data – purpose limitation, retention restrictions and use limitation – neither align with the benefits that can be extracted from data using modern technologies nor are they protecting us against the harms caused by data if it is used without restraint.

The EU has even tacitly acknowledged these shortcomings. Even before the ink dried on the GDPR, it was forced to commence work on a new regulatory framework, one that addressed a range of new areas that data protection regulations do not adequately address.

These new laws, when taken together, constitute the European Digital Strategy and include the Digital Services Act to regulate digital services, the Digital Markets Act to promote fair competition and prevent anti-competitive practices in the digital market, the Artificial Intelligence (AI) Regulation that sets out the legal requirements for AI systems, the Data Governance Act that focuses on data sharing and reuse, and the Data Act to address data access and usage rights. The fact that these new laws are being enacted so fast on the heels of a significant overhaul of Europe's data governance regime is evidence of how futile the European approach has been.

The traditional regulatory approach to data governance is simply not effective enough when it comes to keeping pace with fast-moving technologies. By the time a new data governance legislation is enacted, the technologies it is supposed to govern would have advanced in directions that the law does not address. More importantly, technology companies find it relatively trivial to design their products to skirt around the edges of what is prohibited, using their ingenuity and the plasticity of technology to find gaps in the interpretation of the text, making the regulator's job that much harder with each new evolution of the technology.

Innovators, almost by definition, push the boundaries of what is legally possible. They try and fit their products into the interstices of regulation, building entire business models around the lack of clarity in the law and leveraging regulatory uncertainty into business advantage.

Regulators, hamstrung as they are by laws written at an earlier time, struggle to ensure that innovative business technologies, whose consequences are next to impossible to ascertain, cause as little harm to the users of these products and services as possible. At the same time, they must strike an appropriate balance between too little and too much regulation. Erring too far on the side of light-touch regulation can result in technology companies running amok with no restrictions to curtail their excesses. On the other hand, over-regulating data businesses could leave these industries so strangulated by the knots of compliance that they lose the will to innovate.

These opposing incentives are imperfectly arrayed. Regulators rarely know much about the innovations that businesses come up with until they've been launched, and they often cannot assess the impact an innovation will have on consumers and the market until it achieves scale. If it does cause harm, they come under intense pressure to mitigate these harmful consequences, forcing them to be reactionary rather than measured in their approach.

In a heavily regulated environment, innovators constantly need to stay ahead of new regulations, trying to understand what new legal limits have been imposed on them and how they can re-engineer their technology to achieve their objectives under these constraints. They are constantly tweaking their technology, altering how it functions to ensure that they stay within the realm of the permissible, or at the very least, within the grey zone of uncertainty.

This constant tussle – between regulators and technologists – is a tension as old as technology itself. Modern data technologies have merely exacerbated it. Digital innovators can move faster than ever, building new technologies and scaling them up so rapidly that regulators have scarcely begun to appreciate what they can do before they have grown too large to regulate effectively. And by the time regulators get their act together and come up with what they believe is an appropriate regulatory solution, the technology has evolved again, leaving them eating dust.

The European model of prescriptive regulation has not worked as intended. At the same time, the laissez-faire approach that characterized the early governance of the internet and that, at least in spirit, still permeates through the US approach, has not been a success either. We need an alternative model of governance, one that strikes a balance between these two approaches.

I believe India might have found an answer.

Section 2

India's DPI Journey

Let me tell you the story of Rajani, a young vegetable vendor in Bengaluru, whose story exemplifies India's DPI ecosystem.

Ever since her husband died, Rajani has had to find a way to make ends meet for herself and her young daughter. Life is hard for a single mother in the harsh underbelly of urban India, but with tenacity and more than a little bit of good fortune, she was able to do enough to feed and educate her daughter, if only at a subsistence level. A few years ago, she secured a spot in a crowded street market where she sold a selection of fresh vegetables every morning. Her customers live in the lower-middle-class flats adjacent to the market and, thanks to her pleasant demeanour, tend to seek her out. This means that she is, regularly and increasingly, assured of selling her entire stock by the end of the day.

Rajani's day starts early. She has to get to the wholesale mandi (market) while it is still dark to buy her daily stock and then hurry back to set up shop before the earliest shoppers come by. To do this, she needs to have enough cash in hand, around ₹25,000, to buy the vegetables she will sell during the day. This is a large sum of money for her and even though she knows, with increasing certainty, that every last vegetable in the heap will sell, she has nowhere near the amount of working capital she requires.

And so, before she goes to the mandi, she must stop at a local moneylender who gives her the money she needs – at an exorbitant daily rate of interest.

Rajani knows that her small business is sustainable. That the loan she takes every day will be reliably repaid that evening once she has sold all her vegetables. She has done so every day for over a decade and the moneylender has never once had to unleash his dogs on her. But because there is no way she can reliably prove any of this to the satisfaction of a lender in the formal financial sector, she has no choice but to go to a loan shark for working capital.

Rajani has precisely the sort of business that anyone would love to finance – predictable cash flow, a steady stream of loyal customers and an entrepreneur at the helm who is so personally involved in the business that she is strongly motivated to make a success of it. The problem is that all transactions in the market take place in cash and as a result, even though she nets a small, sustainable profit, she has none of the evidence that a bank needs to sanction a loan. And so she has no choice but to return each day to the moneylender, borrowing what she needs to eke out an existence at interest rates so high that she is barely left with enough to survive.

India's Digital Economy

'Every once in a while, a new technology, an old problem and a big idea turn into an innovation.'

– Dean Kamen

In 2016, Haresh Chawla, a partner at True North, one of India's most experienced and respected private equity funds, wrote an article titled 'How India's Digital Economy can Rediscover its Mojo'. It was a long, well-argued essay about the current state of the Indian digital economy and the new directions it ought to be considering going into. While the entire piece is well worth reading, the unique demographic lens with which he analysed the country was particularly striking to me.

Haresh divides the country by income distribution and wealth into three distinctly different segments. The top 15 per cent of the total population of the country, he points out, earns above ₹20,000 per month and accounts for 60 per cent of the total income distribution of the country. The next 30 per cent earns ₹8,000 per month and makes up only 30 per cent of the total income distribution. The poorest 55 per cent earn just ₹1,500 per month, accounting for only 10 per cent of the total income distribution. In terms of wealth, the top 10 per cent of Indians own 76 per cent of the country's wealth. The next 40 per cent own 20 per cent of the total wealth, while the bottom 50 per cent own just 4 per cent.

As a result, Haresh argues, even though it might seem like we are living in one homogeneous country, there are, in fact, three distinct and almost mutually exclusive Indias coexisting in the same physical territory.

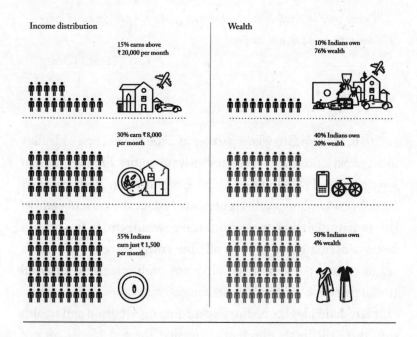

India 1 is the top 15 per cent of the population, accounting for more than 'half the spending power of the economy and almost its entire discretionary spending'. This is the India of the urban elite, those who can afford to go to a fancy restaurant for a meal and travel abroad for a holiday. This is the India that any overseas visitor gets to interact with. And many who live in the elite bubbles of modern India might fool themselves into thinking that this is the only India there is.

India 2 exists immediately adjacent to India 1 but is so well insulated from it that most who occupy this section interact with India 1 transiently at best. That said, about 400 million Indians (more than the entire population of the United States) comprise India 2. These are the people whose job it is to support India 1; they are the ones who earn somewhere in the region of ₹8,000 a month from employment in the service industry, in restaurants and small businesses where they work double shifts to be able to send money back to their families in their villages. These are the Indians who have migrated from the villages to urban areas to improve their lot but are struggling on the periphery of the affluent society that folks in India 1 occupy.

India 3 resides almost entirely in the villages. It comprises 650 million souls who often don't have enough money for two square meals a day. These are the people who have stayed in their villages to tend to elderly family members or to hold on to ancestral land holdings. They are those to whom India 2 sends money when they can. Their lives are so dependent on the harsh vagaries of the monsoon and the erratic munificence of the government that should both of those variables go against them, they will most certainly starve.

If you are reading this book, chances are you belong to India 1. Almost everyone you know – your friends, your family and even most people who work for or with you at office or at home – are also part of India 1. You will come across people who comprise India 2 but rarely. You will interact with them at street markets or the roadside restaurants you might visit or when you hire them to do odd jobs around your home. You will probably never come in contact with India 3 other than seeing them from the window of your air-conditioned car as you whiz past them on highways that, themselves, are increasingly being designed to insulate you from their very existence. Most of us need to make a concerted effort to go deep into the country's rural heartland if we want to interact with India 3.

Rajani belongs to India 2, living as she does in a slum immediately adjacent to the urban elite who make up India 1. Her life is not dissimilar to the 400 million others like her who have insinuated themselves into dark, forgotten corners of Indian metropolises. These are the unfortunate masses which exist in anticipation of the moment when luck breaks in their favour, pulling them out of their penury and into the exalted status of India 1.

Prominently displayed among the neatly organized vegetables in Rajani's tiny roadside vegetable store is a large QR code stuck on a weather-beaten plastic box that has been carefully arranged prominently between the vegetables so that it can be easily scanned by customers using their mobile phones. The QR code contains Rajani's Unified Payment Interface (UPI) payment details, the virtual payment address associated with her bank account.

When a customer scans the QR code, it launches one of several different payment apps on their phone, setting in motion a workflow that opens a payment page pre-populated with the information required to transfer money directly into Rajani's bank account. All the customer needs to do now is put in the precise amount they owe her and press pay. The amount is then transferred directly from their bank account to hers. Rajani gets an almost instant intimation that the amount has been credited to her bank account on her mobile app as well as by SMS.

Rajani cannot read or write, and so she cannot understand the SMS messages she receives confirming that the transactions went through. This is why the box on which the QR code has been printed is so valuable. This is a soundbox, a uniquely Indian innovation that is connected to her UPI account. It announces in a clear, unmistakable voice, in a language that she understands, exactly how much money has just been credited to her account. When she hears this intimation, Rajani knows that the transaction has been completed and she can hand the vegetables over.

When Rajani began to accept digital payments four years ago, she was an oddity in the market. In time, more and more of her customers became comfortable with digital payments and preferred pulling out their phones and scanning her QR code to reaching for their wallets. Today, almost no one pays her in cash.

The use of these digital payments extends to her as well. There was a time when she needed cash for everything – the staples she needed to feed her daughter, the school fees and even the vegetables she bought from the wholesale market. Now, she can complete all those transactions digitally, using her mobile phone. Where, once upon a time, she used to end a successful day at the market with a tinge of fear, knowing that the cash wadded up in the purse she had fashioned out of a corner of her sari made her a target for pickpockets and petty thugs, today, she walks confidently knowing that almost all the days' earnings are sitting in her bank account secured by two factors of authentication.

Data Rich, Economically Poor

When Haresh wrote his article, the effects of digitization were just beginning to make themselves felt. He was confident that India's DPI would make it possible for those in India 2 to avail the benefits accessible at the time only by the top 15 per cent: 'India Stack will craft a new friction-free, lower-transaction-cost highway,' he said, 'that will be accessible on the mobiles of Indians regardless of their income and literacy. It will create a truly integrated market.'

The first part of this vision has come true. Today, smartphone penetration in India 2 is extremely high, and as a result, almost everyone in that segment can access everything India's DPI has to offer. They can open bank accounts and receive benefits directly into the account associated with their digital identity. They can use India's digital payments infrastructure to make all sorts of payments, from sending money to their villages or to buy a cup of tea from a roadside pushcart vendor.

Even a decade ago, people like Rajani had no choice but to accept that it was their fate to remain in India 2. In a world where almost all transactions take place in cash, it is tough to reliably establish a record of the viability of a trading business. As a result, even though her business was fundamentally sound, even though she made enough to cover her expenses and more, there was no way she could prove it to the satisfaction of a formal lender. Thus, Rajani, and countless others like her, have no choice but to go to loan sharks and backstreet moneylenders to finance their businesses.

But over the last decade, a remarkable transformation has taken place. Thanks to the deep penetration of mobile phones in the country, virtually every household has a mobile connection, and every other phone is 'smart'. While most families take advantage of having access to the cheapest data charges on the planet to use these devices for entertainment – watching cricket, Bollywood and OTT serials on a tiny screen shared by many – anyone with a phone can also access India's DPI. Regardless of what the phone is predominantly used for, they have a powerful computer in their pockets that can connect to the internet at any time and use the built-in sensors, cameras and microphones to avail a wide range of services. They can use this device to identify and authenticate themselves, make payments from their bank accounts or receive the money they are owed. They can interact with each other in myriad ways, use it to avail government services and deal with private service providers remotely.

Over the same period, the world has come to realize that there is inherent value in digital data. We have seen how big technology companies leverage our personal information to their advantage in new and evolving ways. We've seen how they use our data to provide content more accurately tailored to our specific preferences and target digital advertisements at us at the precise moment when we are most likely to want to consume them.

If our data can be used in this manner by technology companies to generate value, surely it is possible, trivial even, for that same technology to be used to benefit the poorest among us. If it can generate revenues for the wealthiest companies in the world, can we not use it to extricate the poorest among us from a daily existence that resembles a game of snakes and ladders, where their every move could set off a cascade of consequences that could drive them into penury?

India is the first country in the world to be data rich before it is economically wealthy. Today, 700 million Indians have smartphones and access to some of the cheapest data plans in the world. As a result, vast portions of the population are consuming data and creating, in the process, digital histories that offer deep insights into their habits, behaviours and preferences. We should be able to find a way to interpret the information contained in these digital trails to identify who can be relied upon to repay a loan.

And if we can do that, should we not be able to offer Rajani, and millions like her, a reliable path out of the vicious cycle of poverty?

Having used UPI for her business for four years, Rajani has built a comprehensive digital record of her transactions. She can use this record to demonstrate that her income consistently exceeds her expenses and that she will be able to service any loan that she may take. She always knew this, but it is nice to finally have evidence of it in a form that a formal lender will accept.

To generate this record, all she has to do is go to her bank and ask for a statement. Her branch manager is bound to issue one, providing her an accurate and validly authenticated record of her business transactions, offering lenders proof of the viability of her business. The longer the record she can produce, the more creditworthy she will seem.

The problem is that Rajani does not have the time to do this. Banks are only open during working hours, which is precisely when she needs to be in the market. Her bank documents need to be given to the lender so that the loan officer can evaluate her eligibility. If the first lender she approaches declines her application, she needs to repeat the whole process again and again till she finds someone willing to give her a loan. For someone who lives on her daily sales in the market, she simply cannot afford the effort of getting a loan.

We need a process that allows potential lenders to digitally receive authentic, verifiable information reliably proving Rajani's creditworthiness in a form they can rely on to make their lending decisions. All she needs is for one lender to be convinced that she is worth lending to and that the small business she runs is robust enough to service a loan. One loan, repaid on time, would give her the green shoots of a credit history, her first step into the formal financial system where she can stop turning to usurious lending practices.

Information Collateral

Digital payments have transformed India. Today most retail transactions take place online. From swanky department stores to pushcart vendors, virtually everyone will allow you to pay using your mobile phone. The same is true for services. While all digital services, understandably, have tightly integrated digital payments workflows, even truly offline services – such as tipping a parking attendant or paying a handyman for odd jobs – are done through payment apps. It has got to the point where almost everyone I know cares more about ensuring that their mobile phone is adequately charged when they leave home than about whether they have enough cash in their wallets.

Apart from all the consumer benefits of having a cost-effective digital payment solution that is widely accepted throughout the country, India's digital payment system makes it possible for ordinary citizens to accumulate verifiable and non-repudiable evidence about their activities. Aggregated chronologically, this provides a historical record of their transactions that serves as irrefutable proof of how cash has flowed into and out of their bank accounts over a long enough period to establish their financial credentials reliably. This information would, for many lenders in a competitive market, offer enough evidence of a person's creditworthiness to be able to extend them a working capital facility.

Over the past decade, new classes of non-banking finance companies and fintech companies have emerged, and they have made it their business to target precisely this sort of market – businesses and individuals who fall below the thresholds set by the formal banking system but who are still a solid enough credit risk. While these lenders offer loans at higher interest rates than banks and more traditional financial services entities, their interest rates are still much more affordable than moneylenders and the informal sector. What's more, they prioritize efficiency, offering digital workflows to process and disburse loans as well as a range of different options for repayment.

This new class of lenders opens up a range of options that were previously unavailable to the informal sector. Where once their only option was to approach a local goon with links to the underworld to plead for working capital for their business (usually at criminally high rates of interest), they now have access to far more affordable credit from entities regulated by the central bank. In addition, the simple act of taking a loan from one of these companies will establish a credit history that will serve as their path into the formal financial system. With each passing year, as they demonstrate their ability to service the loan reliably, their credit score will improve, entitling them to more favourable financial products from institutions more centrally located within the hierarchy of the formal financial sector.

Digital Transformation

What Rajani has witnessed through her lifetime is a digital transformation the likes of which few in other countries have seen. Over a decade, India has gone from being a developing country with poor infrastructure and a deep divide between the haves and the have-nots to becoming one of the fastest-growing economies in the world with a vibrant entrepreneurial population.

This transformation has been all the more remarkable for

how little it has cost, given the various challenges that had to be overcome along the way. When India started down this path, it had poor technology infrastructure – low broadband connectivity and smartphone penetration, and all the associated challenges of poor digital access and literacy. The benefits it needed to deliver had to reach over a billion people and support transactions initiated at all levels of the social spectrum. Given the sheer scale of the diversity of this country, it needed to reach people across geographical, linguistic, educational and cultural barriers. And it had to do this at a price that was affordable yet sustainable.

And yet, despite these odds, the transformation has been remarkable. In 2014, just 15 per cent of the population had a smartphone. By 2022, 65 per cent of the country (over 700 million users) had one, and mobile penetration rates had dramatically increased. Over the same period, the cost of data plummeted to about 17 cents a gigabyte (GB), while actual data consumption grew from 0.5 GB a month to 0.5 GB a day.

This rapid digitization led to an unprecedented democratization of access as people from all strata of society could easily access entertainment, commerce and information through their mobile devices. They could also access digital services – identity, authentication, payments, education, commerce – which were now available to everyone at impossibly low costs.

The success of India's digital transformation has much to do with the policy path it chose to build the infrastructure. Instead of recruiting vendors to create the various components of the digital infrastructure, it designed protocols that described open, interoperable digital architectures to provide public services.

This architecture comprised several modular and interoperable building blocks that could be deployed through public–private partnerships and which, when assembled into a digital stack, could provide a range of services for the public benefit at population scale.

I have observed India's digital transformation from the sidelines, watching as the stack has grown from the identity system that started it off with to the point where virtually every sector of the economy has incorporated the DPI approach into the services it provides. I have commented extensively on the legal and regulatory design underpinning many aspects of the stack – from the privacy implications of these systems to the competition and consumer protection measures they advance.

But as I spent more time studying the system, I began to see, hidden within the technical design and operational principles on which these systems were based, a new approach to governance that incorporated legal and regulatory principles into the technical design of the system. Done well, this meant that compliance with the law could be assured merely by participating in the ecosystem.

This is a new approach – one that has not yet been attempted in relation to data governance. It has advantages over the laissez-faire market approach of the US as well as over the regulation-focused approach that Europe has taken for nearly as long. When regulators use technology to govern technology, it makes them more effective, allowing them to see the direct impact of their regulations on the stakeholders they govern. It encourages private participation in the delivery of public services, ensuring that the economy can benefit from private innovation while still guaranteeing sufficient regulatory oversight against the excesses of commercial greed.

Most people view India's digital public infrastructure as a development initiative – a way for countries to leapfrog traditional stages of development using powerful technical infrastructure. But few appreciate the governance implications of this infrastructure and the promise that it holds as an alternative to how we currently regulate our data economy. While it is not a complete solution to all the problems that this economy has thrown up, it is hard to ignore the potential this infrastructure offers in solving some of the more intractable challenges of governance that we face today.

But before we explore that, let us first discuss the different elements of India's DPI – how they work and the functions they were designed to perform. We can then extract a set of governance principles implicit within the DPI framework to evaluate how they can be more universally applied to other systems built in different contexts.

Categories of DPI

'Innovation distinguishes between a leader and a follower.'
— Steve Jobs

When people talk about DPI, they categorize them in several different ways. Some believe that they should be examined sectorally because each industry has different elements that must be considered while building its digital infrastructure. Others look to functional classifications, categorizing them based on the role they perform within the sector they are deployed in and more broadly in the ecosystem. While there is no right and wrong approach, I like to think of the growing catalogue of India's DPI based on the stages of maturity they describe.

When a DPI is first introduced, citizens need a way to *access* it. This is provided through identity building blocks that authorize their use of the ecosystem and the credentials that unlock access to various administrative and other elements. In the financial system, this takes the form of the electronic Know Your Customer (eKYC) systems that are necessary to open a bank account and the other credentials needed to participate in other financial services. In other sectors, there will be similar variants.

Once they have been granted access, participants need to be allowed to *engage* with various aspects of it by using its different features to carry out defined functions. At this stage, they interact with others who have been granted similar access to the digital ecosystem over digital, trails that allow these sorts of engagements. In the financial ecosystem, an example of this would be the digital payments ecosystem that enables participants to pay for goods and services using mobile applications in addition to other digital instruments – e-vouchers, mandates, etc. – as well as other features that make it possible to provide credit in a paperless, presence-less fashion.

Finally, once the various participants have engaged sufficiently with the ecosystem, the accumulated value inherent in the digital trails they have made can be used to *empower* them. It is at this point, when the ecosystem has reached this level of maturity, that the final evolution of the digital infrastructure can be deployed. This is the empowerment layer of the stack and it comprises some of its most sophisticated elements. It is this layer that offers the most significant transformation.

To be clear, this is just one of the many ways in which we can think about DPI to make them easier to understand. I am not suggesting that this should be the only way we think about DPI or that this lens is the most useful in all circumstances. Even as I was writing this chapter, it occurred to me that there were many DPI that could not be slotted easily into any one of the categories I've outlined, no matter how hard I tried, just as there were many others that could easily fit into multiple different categories.

That said, thinking about DPI like this seems a valuable frame of reference if we look to understand how far a country has come in developing its DPI agenda. It provides a framework within which new interventions can be initiated. We know that without enough time being spent on the *access* and *engagement* stages of maturity, it is difficult for the country to maximize any *empowerment* infrastructure it might want to put in place.

But perhaps most importantly, for the purposes of this book, thinking about DPI in terms of whether it brings about access, engagement or empowerment helps us understand the role it can play in governance.

Questions of access tend to be foundational and the principles implicit in these elements capable of having an impact all the way up and down the stack. On the other hand, engagement infrastructure is more transactional, capable of influencing interpersonal relationships and the risks and rewards that come with them. As for the empowerment layer, since it involves the use of citizens' data and information to provide benefits, it encompasses a range of issues pertaining to privacy, individual autonomy and the competitive commercial advantages of big data. Governance principles embedded in this layer will determine how data transactions balance these different pulls and pushes to the benefit of the individual.

The Access Layer

We all know that to use any digital service you must first establish yourself as a new user, distinct from all the others in the system. This allows the system to identify you uniquely so that the features and benefits you are entitled to can be provided to only you. Unlike physical systems that have all sorts of different ways to identify individuals, digital systems rely on identity tokens to differentiate users. In that sense, identity is a necessary and irreplaceable prerequisite for any digital system.

In the context of population-scale government programmes (such as benefits and subsidies), digital identity must be closely enmeshed with attributes of personhood (citizenship, residency and the like) so that your entitlements are not provided to someone else. Most countries establish identity from birth in strong and irrefutable ways that guarantee uniqueness. Where such systems are not in place, additional measures must be implemented to ensure individuality so that benefits for a given person are not diverted to someone else posing as them.

Regardless of how uniqueness is established, digital identity must be interoperable by design. Once created, the identity should be capable of being used across multiple different systems to authenticate a given user so that they can gain access to all that those systems have to offer. This access can be provided either through a foundational identity or through another subsidiary identity system derived from the foundational identity.

Most countries embarking on digitization programs begin their journeys by implementing digital identity systems. These are a necessary prerequisite for some government digital systems, such as the government-to-person payment systems used to transfer benefits and subsidies directly into beneficiaries' bank accounts. But more importantly, it can be used, when legally permitted, to fulfil KYC requirements across a wide range of different services, allowing those who might otherwise not have had the level of documentation needed to access these services the ability to sign up.

Aadhaar

India's digital identity system is called Aadhaar, meaning foundation, an apt description for a component of the digital infrastructure that has gone on to, quite literally, serve as the foundation for India's DPI revolution. Today, Aadhaar covers 99 per cent of the nearly 1.4 billion people in this country. When it was introduced, it was, unlike other identity systems of the time, digital from end-to-end not just in the manner in which the unique identity was issued but also in how the system was used to digitally authenticate users across several different use cases and was combined with other applications to seamlessly integrate its authentication features into third-party workflows.

Aadhaar is a random, sixteen-digit number issued to applicants to identify them uniquely within the vast population of this country. To ensure that every new number is granted to persons not already in the identity database, the system uses biometrics (ten fingers and iris) to uniquely identify, each new applicant.

Once enrolled, Aadhaar number holders can use it to authenticate themselves across several different services (usually in conjunction with another factor of authentication such as their biometrics or, more commonly, a one-time password sent to their registered mobile number). Because of this ability , it is often called the world's first truly digital national identity system.

Much of India's success in designing and deploying its DPI at scale was thanks to some of the early design choices made while designing the Aadhaar system. Even though the mandate was to give every Indian a unique identity, Aadhaar went much further, building an identity system capable of integrating with other digital systems that wanted to leverage its authentication capabilities.

This design decision was a pivotally important decision. It ensured that even though Aadhaar was a self-contained identity system that performed all the functions it was designed to, it was capable of interfacing with other digital products and services, enabling the authentication features inherent in the digital identity to be used by them. This extensibility inherent in the Aadhaar design became a characteristic of every other DPI that came after it, making re-useability a central design feature.

Aadhaar was the first of the foundational layer of a digital infrastructure that provided citizens and other users of these systems the means to access a whole range of different digital ecosystems that were springing up. Initially, the Aadhaar identity itself was used to access different services. In time, as other ecosystems were built in different sectors, a range of derived identities began to be offered using the same design principles as Aadhar. This allowed India to transition from having its citizens use their Aadhaar numbers to identify themselves everywhere to being able to use a different sector-specific identity, depending on the specific service they wanted to avail.

Credentials

While identity is necessary, it is not sufficient for access to all systems. Your identity describes who you are, but it is often necessary to also explain what you are. For instance, to access educational material, it might be necessary to identify who you are and specify which school you study in. To use a medical portal intended to provide services to doctors, it might, in addition to proving who you are, also be necessary to indicate your particular specialization.

What we do – the ancillary attributes of our lives – is described in our credentials. There are numerous circumstances in which this often goes hand in hand with your identity. If we build a digital identity system for access, it makes sense that we should supplement that with a digital credentialing system that will give us an easy way to provide reliable information about 'what' we do to those who need it.

India's system for digital credentials is DigiLocker, a DPI that anyone can use to present to officials who seek it, digital proof of their credentials. DigiLocker is individually associated with a person and allows them to collect and store various different credentials by fetching a digitally signed version of those credentials directly from the website of a government department or institution providing it. Indian students now use DigiLocker to collect and store their graduation or degree certificates from all the colleges they have attended to prove their academic credentials. Disabled persons use it to get their disability certificates from the Department of Empowerment of Persons with Disabilities. Employees use it to maintain their health passbook from the Employment State Insurance Corporation. Vehicle owners use it get a valid digital version of their driving license and vehicle registration number from the Ministry of Road Transport and Highways. And individuals in over twenty states and union territories can get birth and death certificates.

Over 5 billion credentials have been issued to 150 million individuals using DigiLocker. It is now used ubiquitously across the country and widely accepted wherever physical credentials were previously the only way to gain access. If the police ask you to produce your driving license, they are now willing to accept the version stored in your DigiLocker wallet, and the CISF guards who used to demand physical identity proof to allow you into an airport are now happy with digital evidence from your DigiLocker wallet.

During the pandemic, another credential assumed importance – the vaccination certificate. The CoWIN certificate (indicating whether you had taken one, two or an additional booster dose) was necessary to get on to a plane or to gain access to certain facilities. India's vaccine roll out, arguably the largest and most efficient anywhere in the world, bolted onto it the digital infrastructure to generate a digital vaccine certificate that was valid anywhere in the country and most parts of the world. Thankfully, this is one credential that is no longer required. Still, the fact that India could conceptualize and rapidly deploy a new and necessary credential before the first dose of vaccine went into an Indian arm is testament enough to the power of this sort of access layer digital infrastructure, which can be rapidly spun up even in the direst of emergencies.

What Your Digital Identity Unlocks

In 2008, 25 per cent of all Indian adults had a bank account. This was hardly surprising considering that the first step to opening a bank account was proving your identity, and at the time, only one person in twenty-five had a reliable way to do that. By 2014, Aadhaar had been rolled out and the Pradhan Mantri Jan Dhan Yojana (PMJDY) was launched to allow anyone in

India to open a no-frills bank account using their Aadhaar identity information. By the end of 2019, nearly 380 million bank accounts had been opened under the PMJDY, taking the number of Indians with a bank account to almost 80 per cent of the adult population. According to the Bank for International Settlements, what India achieved in just under a decade, would have taken it forty-seven years had it solely relied on traditional growth processes.

Digital systems that offer identity and credential verification can unlock tremendous value in society by enabling users to access services, benefits and other governance features. This allows government entities and other market participants to place greater store on the veracity of the claims made by a citizen, assured by the very design of these systems that the claims are accurate and tamper-free. This is a significant improvement over paper documents which are notoriously easy to forge or modify. But most importantly, since digital identity and credential verification systems are extensible, they can be accessed by market participants, unlocking unprecedented efficiencies.

When Jio launched its new mobile telecom service, it integrated its user onboarding process with the Aadhaar authentication system. As a result, they were able to add new subscribers at the rate of one every four minutes, creating a new world record by enrolling 16 million subscribers within the first month of operations. This would not have been possible without the efficiencies made possible by Aadhaar eKYC. Jio went on to transform the telecom landscape in the country, making a huge bet on mobile data, rolling out the world's cheapest 4G LTE service. As a direct result, concerns around the exclusion risks posed by poor bandwidth and data connectivity were significantly diminished. It is especially fitting that the telecom network that was, because of DPI, able to scale more rapidly than any before it, contributed significantly to the growth of DPI in the country.

Most recently, the efficiencies that these integrations enabled were evident to all who signed up for the new DigiYatra system, which allows air travellers in India to enter the airport and pass through the various checkpoints using only their face as identification. Signing up to DigiYatra is a one-time process that involves connecting the DigiYatra app to DigiLocker to access a traveller's identity information. Once done, there is no need to present your identity information at the airport entry gate or anywhere else within the airport as DigiYatra interfaces with the airport servers to provide the necessary authorizations for access.

The first step towards building population-scale DPI is establishing digital systems that make it possible to access them reliably. A dedicated access layer for the country ensures greater efficiency of the DPI that relies on it as the time and costs of complying with KYC obligations are significantly reduced. It allows the country to build extensible systems that use a shared governance framework for KYC across all the sectors that rely on this core access component.

Once digital access systems like this have been put in place, countries can focus on building the next layer of applications, those that enable users to transact, allowing them to engage with each other and the various market participants connected to the ecosystem.

The Engagement Layer

Once access is enabled, a whole plethora of services can be opened up for digitization. When the government can be sure that users will not be able to take advantage of the anonymity of the internet to set up multiple fake identities to acquire more benefits than they are entitled to, or to ring-fence their assets in tax-remote ways, it can be more confident of providing public services to them online.

There are many benefits to engaging digitally. In the first place, the cost of engagement online is dramatically lower compared to offline equivalents. Paperless interactions allow individuals to save time and the resources of putting together the physical documentation that must be presented to avail a benefit. They also save the recipient the cost of processing and storage. Presence-less transactions remove the requirement for the individual to be personally present to avail benefits, in most instances allowing them to complete these transactions asynchronously using a mobile device. The cost savings in time and resources is immeasurable.

In addition, end-to-end digital systems have numerous other benefits. By offering public officials an entirely digital workflow, they can leverage automation to streamline cumbersome workflows. It also makes it easier to detect fraud and maintain transaction records that are digitally signed and time-stamped and can serve as irrefutable proof of the completion of a transaction.

In addition to enabling interactions between private citizens and public officials, these systems can also enable greater interaction amongst private entities, individuals and businesses alike. By putting universally accessible trusted digital rails in place, they offer different users the opportunity to interact with each other. This extends to several different types of functions, from commercial transactions to health, education and entertainment. But by far, the most popular use of the engagement layer of digital infrastructure anywhere in the world is payments.

Payments

Card usage in India has always been low. The share of card transactions is below 8 per cent of the gross domestic product (GDP), which is, perhaps understandably below that of advanced economies but, surprisingly, also well below that of other comparable emerging market economies. According to a 2016 report by the Reserve Bank of India (RBI), debit cards were predominantly being used at ATMs for cash withdrawals (nearly 90 per cent of the overall debit card transactions in terms of volume and around 95 per cent in terms of value) instead of at point-of-sale terminals for transactions.

At the same time, India was rapidly embracing the mobile internet. As the cost of data crashed, telecom connectivity deepened and the market was flooded with a glut of cheap, feature-rich smartphones, and almost everyone, particularly in urban areas, had access to the internet on a device that could fit into their pockets. The immediate outcome of the confluence of these circumstances was a burgeoning of digital entertainment options for every class of society. In time, however, the scene was set for several dramatic changes in India's payments ecosystem.

The disruption first came in the form of the UPI, India's

instant real-time payment system launched in 2016. UPI integrated legacy payment systems through an open, interoperable digital infrastructure that offered everyone a virtual payment address that served as a proxy bank account. This allowed them to transfer money from one bank account to another without the risk of exposing potentially sensitive financial data. The system operates 24/7 and makes it possible to access funds instantly.

UPI enabled all manner of transactions – from friends looking to split the tab at a restaurant to paying for all sorts of goods and services. As its usage grew, more and more merchants realized that if they could offer UPI as a means of payment, they would be able to attract more customers. This further deepened the penetration of digital payments in the market to the point where today, street vendors of all descriptions set up QR codes to allow customers to pay by UPI.

The COVID-19 pandemic was, in many ways, a turning point for digital payments. In a world where social distancing was the norm and the physical exchange of anything had to be followed by a lengthy ritual of sanitization, cash came to be actively frowned upon. India's robust and tested digital payments ecosystem stepped smartly into the breach, offering those who wanted to avoid touching anything the chance to avoid dealing with physical cash. By the end of 2022, with the pandemic behind us, the UPI ecosystem had scaled up to the extent where it was supporting over 8 billion transactions per month. Its once-fanciful target of processing 1 billion transactions per day was, with every passing day, looking more and more likely.

UPI is the perfect example of DPI designed to support the transactions layer of the country's digital stack. It leveraged the ubiquity of smartphones and created a blindingly simple system that made it as easy as just clicking on the contact you want to transfer the money to (or scanning their QR code) and then authorizing payment. Everything else takes place behind the scenes as the respective banks of the transferor and the transferee, which are connected through the UPI switch, credit and debit the respective bank accounts to reflect the transaction in real time.

More importantly, UPI allowed ancillary ecosystems to flourish and grow. Payments are only one part of most commercial workflows. Now that a large enough number of market participants were actively accepting digital payments, other aspects of the commercial workflow could also be digitized. With several ubiquitous communications options and dozens of micro-delivery services operating in most metropolitan cities, it was possible for all sorts of businesses to provide an end-to-end commercial offering entirely powered by these digital alternatives.

Commerce

When I first heard of the Beckn protocol, it was touted as a mobility service that unbundled the vertically integrated solutions available at the time to enable multimodal transport solutions for users. Today, the Beckn protocol is the technology underpinning the open network for digital commerce (ONDC), which has often been described as India's response to the overwhelming dominance of big e-commerce platforms. But before we start making comparisons, let's understand what the Beckn protocol can do and the alternative that it offers.

A commercial activity, reduced to its most basic terms, is a transaction that takes place between a buyer and a seller. In its simplest form, it takes place in person, with the buyer and seller interacting with each other, such as in a market or department store. The buyer identifies the items they intend to purchase and the seller offers a price at which they are willing to sell it. Once they have negotiated an acceptable arrangement, money exchanges hands and the buyer gathers their purchases and leaves. In an in-person sale, the only element of the transaction that can be digitized is the payment by replacing the physical exchange of cash with a digital payment. As we pointed out, this is already taking place throughout India.

Things get slightly more complicated when the buyer and seller are interacting remotely, for instance, when the buyer calls the local grocer to order some staples and arranges to have them delivered home. Thanks to our digital payments and communications infrastructure, most aspects of this transaction can be completed digitally. The customer can call the grocer or send them a message on WhatsApp with a list of their requirements. Once the order is confirmed, the customer can pay using UPI. What is a little harder is having the purchased item packed for transport and having it delivered.

In many Indian cities, several delivery services – Porter, Dunzo, Delhivery, etc. – have sprung up to fill this gap. Any of them will pick up a package from one part of the city and deliver it, no questions asked, to any other part for a reasonable fee. A customer can complete the transaction and instruct the grocer to hand the package to a delivery person who will deliver it to his doorstep. As simple as this sounds, getting it right is not a simple matter. Ensuring that the grocer hands the correct item to the right delivery person requires some effort, particularly if many other shoppers have had the same idea. Of course, this is far easier to do with a grocer you know and trust than with a random store with which you have no prior relationship.

Beckn attempts to provide a more reliable solution by breaking down the commercial transaction into four constituent elements: search, ordering, payment and delivery. Customers first search through a list of products and services on offer. They then place their order (the equivalent of putting a product in a shopping cart) and make their payment. Once the buyer completes these three stages, the seller arranges for the products to be packed and delivered to the location identified by the customer.

Beckn describes these four stages through a series of interoperable protocols that allows each separate element to be daisy chained together in any number of different configurations so that sellers can implement customized solutions that perfectly suit their desired outcomes.

How would this take place?

First, the vendor needs to convert their entire inventory of products into a digital format. This is then aggregated by integrators (seller apps) whose job is to collect all those products and services into a master list of commodities that will make up their inventory of products. This is how the available inventory of a specific store is presented to potential purchasers. No customer would be able (or willing!) to trawl through the inventories of potentially hundreds of small grocery stores. To simplify the process, seller apps further aggregate these offerings into searchable databases that are presented to potential customers after being sorted by product and location.

Any entity that has goods or services to offer can become a seller on ONDC. Delivery persons willing to deliver products from point A to point B can also list their services on ONDC. A merchant with a confirmed order can engage such a delivery agent to pick up purchased products and deliver them to customers. By stringing services together like this, customers can avail a range of different products and services.

In some of my conversations with the team working on the protocol, I was given the following example. If you need to go to the airport early in the morning and have some coffee too, you could book a taxi and arrange to have a cup delivered to you at a convenient traffic light along the way. ONDC makes it possible for you to process the entire workflow in a single seamless transaction and will manage all the logistics, including working out where the coffee delivery should meet your taxi, so that you have enough time to drink your coffee before you reach the airport.

So is ONDC the big e-commerce killer it has been made out to be?

It is probably too early to comment on this right now. I believe that there will always be a role for full-stack vertically integrated platforms. Their ability to exert control over every stage of the e-commerce pipeline generates efficiencies, better customer experiences and economies of scale that will always appeal to a segment of the market. They will, as a result, always remain relevant. But precisely because of the scale at which they operate, they will struggle to offer the customized service offerings necessary for hyperlocal commerce. This is where I believe ONDC will shine.

While the two examples we've just discussed describe purely commercial applications, the engagement layer has many different applications across sectors. For instance, several different DPI that enable government and citizen interactions could also be included within this layer. This would include the Unified Logistics Interface Platform, a logistics gateway looking to integrate information available with different government agencies into a single platform to provide end-to-end visibility to consumers of the status of their packages, the availability of empty containers and a host of other solutions and services. Similarly, the digital health management ecosystems currently being built by the National Health Authority (NHA) also operate in the engagement layer of the stack, offering a range of data-driven services in the healthcare space.

DPI in the engagement layer is typically most effective when built atop a foundation of access services. The success of UPI would not have been possible if India's national identity programme had not enabled the PMJDY, which, in turn, made it possible for 85 per cent of the adult population to get a bank account. Similarly, the stack of DPI in the health space would not have been possible without the identity and credentialing infrastructure that exists at the foundational access layer.

Transactional layer applications enable the development of other transactional layer applications. Once built, they encourage continuous expansion in the sector and extend their reach by building further digitization into these workflows. Take ONDC, for example. Once UPI made digital payments ubiquitous across the country, it was possible to develop more sophisticated commercial workflows.

The bulk of DPI is established in the engagement layer.

However, once engagement takes place at scale, the digital trails created by such engagement can be further used to their benefit.

For this, a whole new class of DPI will need to be built.

The Empowerment Layer

Arguably the most advanced layer of India's DPI is the empowerment layer as manifested in the Data Empowerment and Protection Architecture (DEPA), a consented data-sharing framework capable of being applied across different sectors. It is here that DPI's ability to function as a new framework for data governance is most apparent.

My first introduction to DEPA was in 2017. I had been invited to participate in a panel discussion when it was being launched, and I couldn't understand why they wanted me there. Based on what I knew then, DEPA was a framework for electronic consent which enabled users to authorize the secondary use of their personal data. As someone who has long worried about the diminishing value of consent as a means to ensure data protection, this sounded like just the sort of techno-utopic solution that would lead to all sorts of problems. That's why those present on the day still recall how distinctly uncomfortable I was participating in the panel discussion.

But after that initial, rather uncomfortable introduction to DEPA, I was determined to give it a fair chance. Rather than relying on what I was being told, I decided to see what it was about for myself. Until then, no lawyer had been associated with its design, and I was willing to consider the possibility that the language used to communicate the concepts imperfectly described how it worked. If I could understand exactly how it was supposed to work, the safeguards built into it and the concerns, if any, with its design, perhaps I could reframe DEPA in language that the data governance community would better understand.

And so, over the next few months, I dug deep into the design of DEPA to try and understand how it worked. I spent time with its designers, insinuating myself into internal discussions and brainstorming sessions till I slowly began to understand what it offered.

I realized, early on, that DEPA was not what I had initially been led to believe. This was not a digital consent framework designed to replace click-wrap contracts. Nor was it an answer to the problems we associate with some of the more egregious data processing practices of social media companies and Big Tech.

It was, instead, aimed at solving a very specific problem, one that not many others had focused upon. It looked to build pipes that connected different data silos to each other and did so through a brand-new institutional intermediary designed for that purpose. These connections would make it possible for users to access information pertaining to them even when that data was controlled by a data fiduciary. It would allow data principals to request the data fiduciary to transfer that specific data from one data silo to another, subject to the principles of purpose specification, data minimization and retention restrictions embedded directly into the technology infrastructure. It was the first digital solution for data portability that I had seen that could be applied to the entire sector.

But first things first. Let's understand how it works.

What DEPA Has Been Designed to Solve

The best way to understand how DEPA works in practice is to go back to Rajani and see how she might use it.

Rajani has had a bank account for four years now. Ever since she linked her account to UPI, she has received payments directly into her bank account from anyone else who is also active on UPI. All her customers need to do is put in their virtual payment address (VPA) into their UPI app and authorize the transfer from their bank account. Once approved, the UPI system ensures that money is debited from their account and immediately credited to hers. Both parties receive confirmation within seconds that the transaction has concluded successfully.

As a result, Rajani has accumulated, in her bank account, a detailed transaction-wise record of all the money that has come into and gone out of her account over the past four years. There is a list of all the payments she has made at the wholesale market every morning when she buys her stock for the day as well as a record of each amount she has received from her customers over the day.

The trouble has always been that this record of transactions is hard to extract from the bank's clutches. It requires a personal visit to the bank and usually comes at a cost. The bank, believing that this transaction history offers it a competitive advantage over others in the market, has every incentive to perpetuate this data asymmetry – knowing that in the hands of a third party, this data could be used to lure their customers away. This is why, even though we have known that a cumulative history of transactions would be a valuable indicator of creditworthiness for a long time, fintech companies looking to compete with banks for customers, have always struggled to obtain it.

DEPA offers a solution that directly integrates into the bank's core technical systems, allowing users granular access to their data, making it possible for specific data fields to be identified and the data within them to transferred with the users' consent.

Using DEPA, Rajani can generate a list of transactions over a specified period and instruct that these be provided to a potential lender. The information will then be collated by the bank, digitally signed and encrypted, and transferred to the potential lender using the rails of the DEPA infrastructure. Even though the process is entirely paperless, the lender can rely on the information because it has been authenticated by the sending bank.

DEPA has made it possible for Rajani (and countless others like her) to access the formal financial system. While the initial loan she receives will be more expensive than one from a bank, it is still much cheaper than the interest she pays to the moneylender. What's more – and this is probably the most important factor – by demonstrating that she can service this loan, Rajani is establishing credit history that will allow her to take other loans in the future. As she continues to build up her reputation, it is only a matter of time before banks will have the confidence to lend to her directly at even lower interest rates.

This, in broad terms, is what DEPA is capable of achieving. With that understanding in place, let's take a look under the hood.

The DEPA Workflow

In the use case described in the previous section, there are essentially three participants in the transaction: Rajani (the user), her bank (the data provider) and the potential lender (the data consumer). If we were to draw a diagram of the transaction, it would look like this:

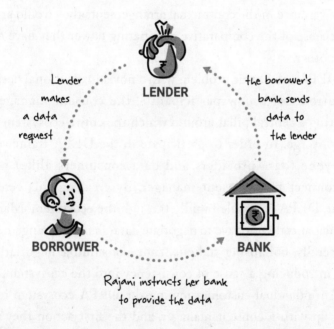

The simplest way to build a digital system to implement the data transfer objective would be to connect all three directly. The user would be able to instruct the data provider to send the required information to the data consumer, who would receive the information directly in their system. This is precisely how banks in Australia are implementing the Consumer Data Rights framework (another attempt to connect data silos to each other to enable data flows). It is being done through a series of bilateral arrangements between entities that have agreed to participate in this data transfer project.

There are, however, several challenges to this sort of approach. In the first place, it is not particularly scalable. Given the number of banks in India, if we had to broker agreements between them, it would take years to scale. In addition, if the banks were to be allowed to negotiate directly with each other, there would be wide variance in the contractual arrangements they would arrive at because of the comparative negotiating power they have over each other.

DEPA solves this problem with a novel institutional design. It introduces a new participant – the consent manager – creating a central pillar around which the entire ecosystem has to converge. In order to participate in the DEPA framework, everyone (data providers and data consumers alike) need to connect to a consent manager. By creating this central pillar, DEPA can scale rapidly through the ecosystem. Market participants do not have to negotiate data-sharing arrangements bilaterally, collapsing tedious, time-consuming negotiations and introducing a sense of consistency into the ecosystem.

An individual customer joining the DEPA ecosystem must sign up with a consent manager, and the first action they will take is to inform the consent manager of the accounts they have with different participants in the financial ecosystem that they might want to connect to the consent manager to transfer their information to a data consumer.

The consent manager achieves one more purpose. Since all consent requests are processed through them, users have a single dashboard on which they can view all the consent requests that they have approved. This would not be the case if the various participants in the ecosystem had bilaterally negotiated data-sharing arrangements.

All this will become clearer as we pick apart a typical transaction on the DEPA framework. But first, let's take another look at how the workflow diagram appearing earlier in this chapter changes with the addition of the consent manager.

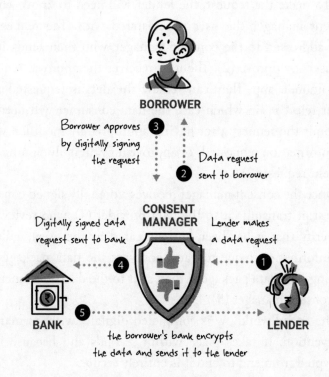

As you can see, the user has been shifted to the top of the diagram and replaced by the consent manager. Both the bank (the data provider) and the lender (the data consumer) are connected to the consent manager. The arrows indicate the sequence of steps describing the process in which a data transfer will occur.

Most data requests are initiated by the data consumer. When

a user approaches a lender for a loan, the lender will ask for certain information to evaluate the user's creditworthiness. In the DEPA system, this request is made in the form of a digital consent request that sets out the types of information requested with details about the time period for which the information needs to be made available and other relevant information (1). To make the request, the lender will need to know which consent manager the user is registered with. The request is then addressed to the consent manager, who then sends it to the user to approve (2). The user receives the approval request on a mobile app. They can review the details requested and either reject it (in which case the data consumer will need to resubmit the request after having appropriately modified with the information requested) or approve it by digitally signing the consent request (3).

Once the consent manager receives a digitally signed consent request, it transmits it to the data provider (4), who reviews it (to verify that it has been authenticated by the user), collates the information requested and encrypts the data package for sending. The data package is then sent to the data consumer via the consent manager (5).

The entire workflow is completed digitally with no manual intervention. It takes place within seconds and because it is encrypted from end to end it is entirely secure.

In addition, the consent manager is data blind by design. In other words, even though the consent manager knows which data consumer is making the transfer request and which data provider is making the data available, it has no idea what data is being transferred by the data provider to the data consumer.

On 2 September 2021, the first DEPA implementation went live in the Indian financial sector. It was called the Account Aggregator ecosystem, and when it launched, only eight private sector banks were signed on to it. In less than a year, with every public sector bank on board, 1.1 billion bank accounts were connected to it. Though very few realized it at the time, this was the largest open-banking roll out in history.

By the end of 2022, nearly ₹17 billion worth of loans had been disbursed through the Account Aggregator framework. More than half of these were disbursed to micro, small and medium enterprises (MSMEs) and were less than ₹4,00,000 in value. These loans would not have been sanctioned had it not been for the DPI that offered alternate signals of creditworthiness for the borrower and enabled dramatic cost reductions.

The banks and financial institutions participating in these transactions reported zero fraud on all DEPA-enabled transactions – the direct digital transfer of financial information from one financial sector entity to another had almost entirely eliminated the risk of forgeries (that previously ranged from anywhere between 0.5 and 4 per cent of all lending transactions).

Some banks reported a rise in loan generation of as much as 30 per cent on a month-on-month basis after going live on the DEPA ecosystem. Others confirmed that the cost of processing had come down from approximately ₹440 per loan to about ₹90. From these early metrics, there is a clear indication that this, the latest in India's long line of digital innovations, is likely to be as successful as those that preceded it.

The transformative effects of India's digital technology revolution are now more than evident. There is a multiplier effect to the incremental innovation it fosters that might be hard to identify in the initial stages, but which becomes apparent as the system operates over time and gains scale. In the recent past, this has been further accelerated by developments in artificial intelligence – in particular large language models and generative AI – that have demonstrated how even more benefits can be unlocked for those parts of the population otherwise beyond our reach.

India's DPI approach is now being cited, with approval, around the world. For many developing countries, it is the only viable path to progress, allowing them to leapfrog traditional cycles of development. Even developed nations, where many of the challenges that their DPI was designed to address are already solved, can leverage the concepts inherent in the design of these frameworks to address first-world problems such as fair competition, urban governance and the like.

But it hasn't all been smooth sailing. From its very inception, concerns have been raised about the path down which India chose to proceed and the harms that could result from an over-reliance on technology. Some of these questions stem from a distrust of technology solutions and the government implementing these systems. Others raise concerns about the impact that these investments in digital ecosystems will have on global challenges like climate change. These are questions we must engage with if we want to hold this approach up as a model for the rest of the world to follow.

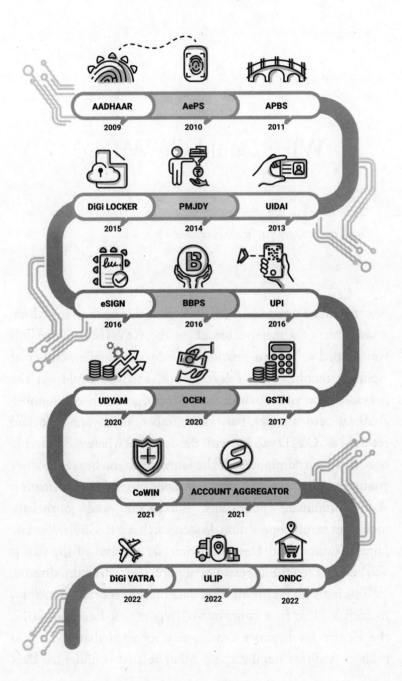

What Could Go Wrong?

'Technology . . . is a queer thing. It brings you great gifts with one hand, and it stabs you in the back with the other.'

– C.P. Snow

Shortly after I turned in the first draft of this book to my editor, news broke of a massive breach of the CoWIN database. All you needed to do was provide the relevant mobile number or Aadhaar number to a Telegram bot, and you could get the personal information (name, date of birth, gender, phone number, Aadhaar card number, passport number) of anyone who had received a COVID vaccine with the details of where their vaccine dose had been administered. The journalists who broke the story confirmed that the bot could provide verifiable information about prominent politicians, bureaucrats and journalists, including senior opposition leaders such as P. Chidambaram, Jairam Ramesh and Derek O'Brien. By the end of the day, it was being called the largest 'digital public infrastructure' disaster.

This is, by no means, the first data breach reported in relation to India's DPI. In a controversial report first issued in 2017, the Centre for Internet and Society reported that about 130 million Aadhaar numbers and other related confidential data had accidentally been made public. A year later, the *Tribune* broke the news that an anonymous WhatsApp group was selling Aadhaar card details for ₹500 a pop. In 2019, the Hyderabad police lodged an FIR against IT Grids Pvt. Ltd for having 78 million Aadhaar records from Andhra Pradesh and Telangana in its possession. These had presumably been obtained from the State Resident Data Hub. In 2021, a hacker group called Red Rabbit obtained access to the records of 2.5 million Airtel customers, including their Aadhaar numbers, addresses, dates of birth, names and phone numbers. In 2022, a security researcher was able to access a portion of the Pradhan Mantri Kisan Samman Nidhi website that revealed the Aadhaar information of the 100 million farmers registered on it.

As more and more of our data goes online, information previously stored in physical files is now increasingly available online. That data accumulates and if breached, it could result in the public disclosure of information about our financial well-being, the state of our health and a host of other data that we would rather everyone did not know. In extreme cases, malicious actors could use this to access our accounts and digitally siphon away our hard-earned money.

It is, therefore, important to discuss what could go wrong with the widespread digitization of society. As we commit to DPI, extending it to more and more sections of society, it is important to be aware of these risks so that even if it is not possible to eliminate them, we must at least mitigate their impact through the careful design of our digital systems.

In an earlier chapter, we categorized the concerns brought about by digital systems into three basic categories – breach of privacy, surveillance and automated decision-making. In the Indian context, while we have yet to see widespread use of automation in decision-making, there are certainly concerns around the risk of exclusion brought about by deploying these digital interventions.

Let us examine each of these concerns separately.

Breach of Privacy

The most common consequence of greater digitization is the increasing concentration of data in the hands of individual service providers. As more and more service providers move their offerings online, more and more aspects of our daily lives – previously recorded physically in files – are being captured digitally and stored in the cloud. Malicious actors, who previously had to find ways to access individual stores of data, can now target these vast stores to access information about us and millions of people like us.

Is the push towards greater digitization worth the risk? If, as a result of deploying DPI, we are increasing the chances of our personal data being accessed by those who can use it to harm us, should we be going down this path at all?

Considering the many benefits that digitization has to offer, it appears that most countries have evaluated these risks and concluded that they are worth taking. Today, it is no longer a question of whether we should embrace digital technologies but of how. All digitization increases the risk of data breaches. As a result, in most instances, it is no longer a question of whether we should risk going down the path of digitization but instead of assessing what the acceptable level of risk is. In evaluating the privacy consequences of adopting the DPI approach, the question we must ask is not whether it exposes us to the risk of a data breach but whether that risk is worse than the risks that other approaches to digitization present.

In terms of timing, news of the CoWIN data breach could not have come on a more inopportune day. Just that morning, the G20 Digital Economy Working Group had convened in Pune for their third meeting of the year. High on the agenda was cybersecurity and the adoption of India's DPI approach. A few countries – Armenia, Suriname and Sierra Leone – were scheduled to sign memorandums of understanding (MoUs) with the Government of India to learn from its experience of using technology to improve governance and potentially deploy India's DPI approach to effect digital transformations in their countries.

When I first heard of the breach, I was aghast. My endorsement of the DPI approach was based on the assurance that everything possible had been done to ensure that citizens' data was adequately secured. I knew, from personal experience, that the only way I could access my own CoWIN data was by providing a one-time password that was sent to my registered mobile phone and was only valid for 180 seconds. To gain access to my information, a hacker would have to find a way to get to that information without physically possessing my mobile phone.

By the time I was able to use the Telegram bot, it was no longer providing access to the CoWIN data. But from the screenshots posted online, it looked like the bot was only providing a subset of CoWIN information. This suggested that even if this data was being extracted live from the CoWIN database, some intermediate work was being done on it before it was being offered up by the bot. If the data was being reformatted before it was made available via the bot, who was to say that it was not being embellished by additional data from elsewhere?

By the end of the day, questions were being raised about whether the breach was, in fact, all that it had been portrayed to be. Reporters from *India Today*'s open-source investigation team claimed to have contacted the hacker, who admitted that the results generated by the chatbot were accessed using a vulnerability in another platform associated with the Health Ministry. Apparently, he had used this portal to access the details of an auxiliary nurse midwife and, thereafter, the data was delivered by running a query via Telegram. Perhaps most significantly, he confirmed that there was no mass data dump of the CoWIN data. Instead, he exploited a vulnerability that allowed him to retrieve individual data of people whose phone numbers or Aadhaar numbers were available. This was corroborated by the statements of the Government of India that whatever the bot was doing, it was not accessing the CoWIN database in real time.

If the hacker did not have access to the actual CoWIN data, allegations as to the size of the data breach were no longer accurate. While there is no getting away from the fact that no amount of personal information should make its way into the hands of malicious actors, confirmation that the entire database was not exposed provides a (albeit small) measure of comfort.

Most data breach incidents in India tend to be reported in hyperbolic terms. In 2017, the Centre for Internet and Society had to publish a clarification to its report on the information security practices of Aadhaar: 'The term "leaks" was originally used twenty-two times in the report,' they said. '[T]his has led to reports that security measures on these portals were compromised. However, the intention behind the publication of this sensitive data was greater transparency, and no access control measure was in place. Therefore, this is best characterized as an illegal data disclosure or publication and not a breach or a leak.' This clarification, welcome as it was, came a little too late. By that time, newspapers around the country had referenced the report as evidence of the vulnerability of the identity database, a stain that would never be washed away.

The *Tribune* report on the breach of Aadhaar data had even more significant consequences. Its allegation that identity information of Indian citizens was available for as little as ₹500 led the World Economic Forum to state, in its *Global Risks Report 2019*, that the largest data breach of the year had taken place in India, 'where the government ID database, Aadhaar, reportedly suffered multiple breaches that potentially compromised the records of all 1.1 billion registered citizens.' As one would imagine, this significantly shaped global perceptions of the security of the information in India's digital infrastructure.

As a matter of fact, the *Tribune* was able to get hold of Aadhaar data through a search facility incorporated into the design of the Aadhaar infrastructure to allow authorized government officials to access the database to rectify mistakes in the spelling of a citizen's name. This was a facility only available to government officials, and the fact that a search service was being made available for a price on a WhatsApp group suggests that a rogue government servant was misusing their privileges. Instead of the entire database of 1.1 billion data records being out in the wild as was suggested, an individual who had been granted access to the database was misusing that privilege to share demographic information corresponding to each individual Aadhaar number they had been provided. This is not unlike your bank teller sharing information about your financial status without your consent. No amount of system design will be effective against the determined efforts of rogue administrators looking to subvert it.

In their reporting of data breach incidents, journalists tend to exaggerate the implications of the news they are breaking. I can't tell if this is because of a genuine lack of understanding of how the technology works or because sensationalism drives readership. This is why I have made it a point never to comment on a breach incident as soon as it happens. I wait instead for the facts to surface before commenting. More often than not, closer investigation reveals that what was billed as a massive data breach was nowhere near as bad as it was made out to be.

But any data breach, no matter how small, affects those whose data has been exposed. Even if that number is just a tiny subset of the total database, the harm caused to them is real and cannot, in any way, be diminished. Where this is directly attributable to deficiencies in the DPI to which this data was entrusted, it deserves serious attention.

Thankfully, most incidents of data leaks that are, even tangentially, associated with India's DPI have only resulted in the exposure of basic demographic information – name, age, address, gender – and in certain circumstances, Aadhaar, passport and mobile numbers. As bad as this is, it could have been much worse. Around the world, examples abound of data breaches in which highly sensitive information leaks into the public domain, allowing anyone from the dark web to use it to access others' accounts (username and passcode), financial information (bank account and credit card details) or health records (personal medical information). Very few incidents of this nature have, so far, been reported in India.

That said, even this basic demographic data can be used to cause harm. In many instances, these personal details are the security questions users are asked to answer when they want to reset their passwords or access their account through a customer helpdesk. It is a relatively trivial matter for a malicious actor possessing this information to use it to access a user's bank account – or worse. Even if they are not, in and of themselves, particularly harmful, in the hands of the sufficiently motivated, this data can be used as tools of social engineering to compromise our most personal information. There have been reports of elderly citizens who are not tech-savvy being duped by bad actors calling them and using such data to pretend to be bank employees, persuading them to provide more details like passwords or one-time passwords.

It is impossible to completely eliminate the risk of data breaches. Digital systems are complex constructs made up of many parts. Vulnerabilities in the smallest of them could compromise the entire system. Since individual components get upgraded at various different times, the risks they pose tend to change dynamically. What's more, all digital systems have human operators who perform the tasks that machines cannot. These individuals may be easily suborned or duped and convinced to misuse their privileges to disclose information that they are prohibited, by law, from sharing.

If we cannot eliminate these risks completely, it is important to ensure that we have put measures in place that mitigate them to the fullest extent possible. If demographic information can be used to socially engineer access to protected systems, additional layers of protection through the use of multi-factor authentication should be implemented. If no digital system is ever completely immune from compromise, we need to organize our data such that any breach can compromise no more than a small subset of the total data set. Any evaluation of the security of India's DPI should be made according to these measures.

But a breach of the personal data contained in digital systems is not the only risk these systems pose to personal privacy. Far more pernicious is what this information could reveal about us. As digital systems insinuate themselves deeper and deeper into our lives, the information we share with them is increasingly likely, particularly in the hands of a repressive government, to be used to harass and persecute us. And as more and more of these interoperable systems are built and connected to each other, the easier it becomes for those who can control them to infer insights about us that might otherwise not have been easily discernible.

Unless we explicitly mitigate it through design, greater digitization inevitably increases surveillance risks.

Surveillance

In July 2021, a network of global media organizations and civil society organizations revealed that governments around the world had been using Pegasus, a software developed by an Israeli firm called NSO, to carry out advanced surveillance on certain individuals. The software installed itself in the mobile phone of the target and then, from within the operating system, eavesdropped on calls, read messages, accessed social media activity and captured their browsing history. Since it was effectively installed as an application on the device, it could elude the protection offered by end-to-end encryption and the other defences commonly deployed to defend against intrusion.

In the list of the individuals around the world who had been surveillance targets using this software were over 170 Indians, including sitting ministers of the government, leaders of the opposition, journalists, members of the legal community, businessmen, assorted government officials, scientists and human rights activists. Such was the public outcry that ensued from these revelations that the Supreme Court of India took it upon itself to set up a panel to look into the veracity of these allegations.

As shocking as it might have been to learn that the government was intruding so deeply into the personal lives of its people, this was only the most recent evidence of the ever-expanding use of digital technologies in domestic surveillance. Similar concerns had previously been raised about the Central Monitoring System (CMS), a technology that allowed investigation agencies to directly intercept phone calls without asking a telecom service provider and NatGrid, the integrated intelligence network designed to connect the databases of different Indian security agencies so that patterns from the data produced could be surfaced in real-time for use by national security agencies.

To be clear, India is in a precarious geopolitical situation, surrounded by hostile nations with whom it has a long and relatively unbroken history of conflict. It has been subject to numerous acts of terrorism that have caused death and destruction in some of its most populous cities. Because of this ever-present threat, security agencies in the country operate with a heightened sense of risk, ever on alert for intelligence of potential acts of aggression so that they can take pre-emptive steps to mitigate loss to human life and property. If technology interventions can help in this regard, few will argue that the resulting loss of civil liberty is not a worthwhile trade-off.

However, once built, digital surveillance tools are often deployed for purposes other than national safety – to snoop on political adversaries, journalists with avowedly anti-government leanings, or others simply because their views do not align with those who have the power to order such use. In any democratic country, this would be considered outside the purview of the national security exemption.

This is why the public outcry in response to the Pegasus revelations was so strong. Even to the casual observer, it was obvious that many on the list posed little or no risk to national security. The fact that they had been the subject of such intrusive and indiscriminate surveillance suggested that the government was willing to use digital technologies to achieve narrow political ends.

It is these concerns that have led so many to look askance at India's DPI. Any government that has no qualms about using digital tools like Pegasus to spy on ordinary citizens could hardly be expected to refrain from redeploying its population-scale digital systems to achieve similar ends – particularly when such significant portions of its populace have been enrolled in and are actively using these systems. These are concerns that have dogged the deployment of DPI in India from the very beginning.

When the government announced that it was going to create a unique digital identity for all Indians, I must admit that this was the first thing that occurred to me. I worried that a unique digital identity would allow the government to know more about its people than perhaps it could be trusted to.

In an earlier book, I told of how I shared these concerns with Nandan Nilekani, then the chairman of the Unique Identification Authority of India (UIDAI) and impressed upon him the need to enact a privacy law to establish a governance framework within which the unique identity project should operate. Absent this, I feared that the privacy implications of an undertaking of this magnitude would end up raising such deep fundamental rights concerns that it would place the entire project in jeopardy. To his credit, Nandan got the point immediately and did what he could to get the government to enact appropriate legislation.

One of my chief concerns was that a ubiquitous digital identity with the high level of assurance that Aadhaar provided would eliminate the fuzziness that characterized our social interactions at the time, allowing anyone at the right vantage point to learn things that we would have preferred remained private. I worried that as more and more services incorporated this identity into their workflow, it would clear the fog that surrounded our various activities, making it easier and easier to piece together who we are and what it is we do.

I worried Aadhaar could be a unifying technology that served as a central spine to which all manner of information about an individual could be attached, building, in the process, a patchwork quilt of information about us that could be used to keep tabs on what we do. As it was linked to more and more services – tax filings, bank accounts and mobile phones – I worried that it would be a trivial matter for some great tech czar in charge of all of these diverse systems to piece together our every movement simply by aggregating the data associated with Aadhaar.

What I did not fully appreciate at the time was that because of how India's DPI had been designed, this was harder to do than one might think. Every service that identifies or authenticates you using your Aadhaar adds your unique identity number to their databases, not the other way around. When you link your bank account to Aadhaar and give the bank your Aadhaar number, the UIDAI does not receive any information about where you bank. If you have obtained a mobile connection using Aadhaar eKYC, the telecom company that enrolled you as a subscriber has your Aadhaar number, but UIDAI has no information about which telecom service you are using. This is true of every other service that you have accessed using Aadhaar, from the hotel you gave a photocopy of your Aadhaar to when you checked in or the security personnel at the airport to whom you gave your Aadhaar card for inspection. If someone wants to build a profile about you using the services associated with your Aadhaar number, there is no central database they can visit to get this information. They will, instead, have to go to all those different databases and extract data associated with your Aadhaar one at a time. This is easier said than done.

Similar concerns have been expressed in relation to all of India's DPI. Digital payment systems can provide insights about what we spend our money on – the products we buy and the services we consume are clear indicators of our personality and preferences. Healthcare systems will know what ails us – be it a life-threatening disease or simple vanity about hair loss. Commercial infrastructure will understand what makes us tick. If any of these systems accumulate this information about us into a central database, it could offer unprecedented insights into who we are and what we do. If connected to each other, those who control that central database would know us better than we know ourselves.

As it happens, almost all of India's DPI have been designed to be optimally federated, leaving data at the edges where it was created rather than being aggregated into centralized storage systems. This makes it that much harder for the data in these digital systems to be used for surveillance, forcing those seeking to use it like that to go from database to database to piece together the profile they want.

Over the past few years, I have had occasion to discuss India's DPI with experts around the world to enlighten them about all that we have achieved and to show them how these DPI could be deployed in developing countries to leapfrog traditional stages of development. In all these sessions, the one question I am invariably asked is what will happen if these population-scale digital ecosystems are deployed by repressive regimes. Would you not worry, they often ask, that you are providing dictators with the tools with which to amass intelligence on their people and potentially persecute them?

My answer has always been twofold. In the first instance, precisely because the Indian approach to DPI implements optimal federation, it makes it difficult for any one entity to use it to build a digital panopticon. If that were their real intention, the regime would be far better off hiring vendors to design monolithic centralized systems than opting for DPI. Countries that adopt the DPI approach are, through that very act, committing themselves to the democratic values embedded within these systems.

Secondly, since these systems are modular and interoperable, every subsequent item of digital infrastructure layered upon the foundational DPI reinforces the principles of those before it. Over time, as more and more DPI is layered onto the stack, the harder it becomes to redefine how elements at the base of the stack perform. Eventually, there will come a point when even if an oppressive government takes over, it will be next to impossible for them to use the existing infrastructure for repressive ends because of how deeply democratic principles are embedded into the foundational elements of the stack.

Surveillance is an overt act that requires governments to take specific steps to make these digital systems yield their desired outcomes. Well-crafted DPI can make it difficult for repressive regimes to subvert the original purpose of these systems by embedding democratic principles directly into the technical design.

But there are other, far less overt ways in which population-scale digital systems can cause harm. In many parts of the world where digital systems are being deployed, connectivity is patchy, leading to zones in which access to these systems is poor or non-existent. The sections of society that these systems are intended to reach often cannot afford the smartphones needed to avail the benefits that they provide. Even if they have access to the device, they often lack the digital literacy required to safely use it. If care is not taken to appropriately account for these issues, the benefits these systems were designed to deliver will not be fully realized.

Exclusion

In 2017, the Jharkhand government cancelled more than 1 million ration cards claiming that they were bogus because they had not been associated with an Aadhaar number. While it is likely that a good number of those cards were, in fact, fraudulent – either completely fake or belonging to a dead person whose family was using it to collect more than was their due – at least some of these cancelled cards belonged to the poor and underprivileged who depended on these rations for survival.

Santoshi Kumari was a young girl in Karimati, a rural village in the heart of Jharkhand. On 20 September 2017, her family ran out of food – the card they had relied on for food grains had been revoked because it was not linked to an Aadhaar number, and they had no other means to get what they needed to survive. For eight days, they went without food, unable to beg or borrow it from neighbours. At 8 p.m. on 28 September, Santoshi complained of a stomach ache. Two hours later, she was dead.

In October 2017, Ruplal Marandi died in the Deoghar district of Jharkhand when his family was denied food grains because their biometric authentication failed. In December that year, Etwariya Devi, a sixty-seven-year-old widow from the Garhwa district, died of starvation, reportedly because an Aadhaar-enabled point-of-sale machine couldn't authenticate her daughter-in-law's biometrics.

According to a list compiled by activists Reetika Khera and Siraj Dutta, a good portion of the hunger-related deaths recorded in 2017 and 2018 were on account of failures in the Aadhaar system. Earlier that year, the Jharkhand state government had required these databases to be seeded with the beneficiary's Aadhaar details to eliminate all those who were taking more than they were entitled to. In the process, they excluded many who depended on what they received from ration shops to survive.

These shocking stories are stark reminders of what exactly is at stake when we undertake these massive digital transformation projects. All technology systems take time to get up to speed. The real-world integrations that work so perfectly in the controlled environs of the laboratory struggle to cope with the challenges of the real world and the unpredictable nature of human interactions. In the process, real people suffer in the most horrible ways.

No technology is ever error-free. We can, at best, aspire to perfection, recognizing that circumstances unforeseen and unforeseeable, can and *will* bring our best-laid plans to naught. We need to make allowances for this, building fallback arrangements for situations where the technology does not perform as promised. This is particularly important in the early stages of a new technology, when a combination of teething problems and human administrators coming to grips with how to operate new systems can result in avoidable exclusions. We cannot, in the process of eliminating ghosts from our database, make ghosts of those who depend on those systems.

Unfortunately, this is what happened in the early days of Aadhaar. In many states, Aadhaar-based initiatives were rolled out before everyone in the population to which they applied was completely enrolled. As a result, citizens who were legitimately entitled to benefits were denied them because they had not yet enrolled in Aadhar or were yet to associate their digital identity with the benefits scheme. In other instances, inexperienced administrators, only just beginning to understand what the technology could do, brusquely ignored those they should have been more compassionate to. This was coupled with and compounded by the teething problems of a new technology infrastructure. It is on account of this unfortunate combination of circumstances that there were so many instances of exclusion in the early days of Aadhaar. Thankfully, over time, things have gotten better.

There are broadly two types of exclusion: (i) that which is brought about because of an inability to access the system, either due to a failure to enrol into the service or, once enrolled, to authenticate oneself to avail benefits; or (ii) that which comes from the inability to engage with the technology, either because the device used to avail the service is unaffordable, or the infrastructure on which it relies is unavailable, or because the technology itself calls for skills that the user does not possess. Let us examine these cases to see how relevant they are in India today.

By now, almost everyone in India has an Aadhaar number. With over 1.37 billion numbers issued, the argument that large swathes of the population are being denied access to services because they are unable to enrol themselves for an Aadhaar number no longer holds water. What's more, since its inception, Aadhaar has been used for authentication over 90 billion times, indicating that this system works well and does so regularly at least 50 million times a month. To be clear, this is not to suggest that the machine does not sometimes still struggle to recognize our fingerprints – we often have to try repeatedly before it recognizes our biometrics. What we do know is that the technology does work – even if it takes some time.

Even though most of the country has been blanketed with robust telecom infrastructure, significant gaps remain due to difficulties in terrain, particularly for residents of the Northeast and other inaccessible mountainous and heavily forested regions not easily served by terrestrial mobile networks. In many other parts of India, the connectivity required for these digital systems to run smoothly is patchy at best. This results in a different kind of exclusion, one where the denial of services is on account of a failure of the basic infrastructure that these technologies need to work.

India also has the dubious distinction of ordering the internet to be shut down at the drop of a hat, often when students and ordinary citizens need them the most. According to Access Now, in 2022 alone, 84 of the 187 global internet shutdowns took place in India. For a country that is consciously shifting more and more of its service provision online, the non-availability of internet access will seriously affect citizens who depend on it for their livelihood.

That said, offline capabilities have been baked into most of India's DPI, enabling basic functionality even when the internet is unavailable. Aadhaar verification through QR codes returns digitally signed demographic information about the Aadhaar number holder sufficient for most authentication purposes. UPI QR codes are widely used to transact, allowing merchants to receive money into their accounts even when they don't have a smartphone or their battery has drained and their device switched off.

When India started its DPI journey, there were barely 300 million smartphones in the country, most concentrated among the urban elite. These devices were expensive and largely unaffordable by the masses. Today, there are 750 million smartphones in India, with virtually every household having at least one. Thanks to falling prices and rising demand, these devices have penetrated deep into the country. What's more, many of the services that were once only available through a touchscreen interface are now available on feature phones too, using the USSD protocol through UPI's *99# service. This means that not only can the 750 million smartphone users avail of the service, all the 1.17 billion mobile telecom subscribers in the country can as well.

Finally, there is the question of capacity. The argument most naysayers make is that it takes considerable skill to use DPI, requiring users to display a higher degree of literacy both in terms of the ability to read and write as well as to operate electronic devices – these are beyond the capacity of many. After over a decade and a half of deployment, it is clear that we either underestimated the capacity of ordinary people to adapt to new digital systems, or we overestimated the complexity of the technology. While there are stray examples of the elderly and poor struggling to understand how to use these systems, we have, for the most part, seen that these instances are temporary and that of all the many situations in which exclusion occurs, this is the least likely.

⌐

In the recent past, I have been increasingly called upon to engage in questions pertaining to how the widespread adoption of DPI will impact our commitments to mitigating the harmful effects of climate change. For the most part, these questions have arisen out of a concern that the more we commit to the digital approach, the greater will be our investment in servers and associated paraphernalia, the climate consequences of which have already been well documented.

The fact is that India's DPI approach is not your typical digitization endeavour. It does not call for server farms and massive data centres to be established or huge investments in energy infrastructure. All it does is prescribe the protocols, systems and organizational measures that unlock efficiencies and deliver citizen-centric outcomes. If anything, by establishing the digital architecture that makes it possible for data to flow between parties who need it, pretty much on-demand with the consent of the user, corporate entities will realize that there is no need for them to create their own data silos because they can easily access the information they need whenever they want.

Taking Stock

India's DPI has allowed it to make tremendous progress, taking a massive jump past the traditional stages of development to accelerate financial inclusion. It has managed to enrol the bulk of its population into the formal financial system in less than a decade, a feat that would have taken five decades to achieve if done conventionally. When the DPI was first being rolled out, many worried about the resultant harms. They feared that an over-reliance on technology would result in the violation of our personal privacy, unjustified mass surveillance and technology-enhanced exclusion. But while there have been instances when these harms have befallen some, things are nowhere near as bad as we thought they would be.

The exclusion we worried would take place was less extreme than we feared. Instead, these digital interventions have enabled new ways in which services can be accessed, offering new forms of paperless, presence-less interaction that unlock value in unexpected ways. As a result, India's DPI approach is being widely acclaimed as a solution for many of the development challenges that countries around the world are grappling with.

But India's DPI approach does more than just bridge

development gaps. Contained within its design are features that regulators and policymakers alike can use to fashion new solutions for some of the most difficult data governance challenges. It offers a middle path between the laissez-faire regulation approach on the one hand and a regulation-heavy approach on the other.

This techno-legal approach to data governance is expressed through the design principles that underpin Indian DPI, the legal constructs embedded in its code and the organizational structure of the institutions that are responsible for many different aspects of its functioning. To understand how this new approach works, we need to look at India's digital public infrastructure framework through three very different lenses.

First, we need to look at the core design principles upon which India's digital infrastructure was built. While the primary purpose of these principles is to ensure that India's digital ecosystem is built in an efficient and internally consistent manner, understanding how they function can give regulators new tools with which to embed regulatory outcomes into technology design.

It is also possible to do this explicitly – to encode legal principles directly into the technology architecture. The DEPA framework, India's consented data transfer architecture, has done just that, embedding core principles of data protection into the design of its code. When legal obligations that are typically enforced through statutes can be encoded into technology architecture, participants in the ecosystem will comply simply by using it.

Finally, we need to examine the roles and responsibilities of different participants in the ecosystem so that by carefully arraying opposing interests against each other, no one participant can gain an advantage over any other. By assigning participants in the ecosystem different roles depending on their specific motivations, it is possible to incentivize them to perform in ways that align with policy objectives.

If policymakers can learn how these levers work, they will be able to use them to shape governance outcomes. Using this knowledge, they will be able to design new DPI to achieve new objectives and fine-tune existing systems to continue to deliver the outcomes they were intended for.

An understanding of how these elements work will define India's new approach to data governance.

Section 3

A New Model of Data Governance

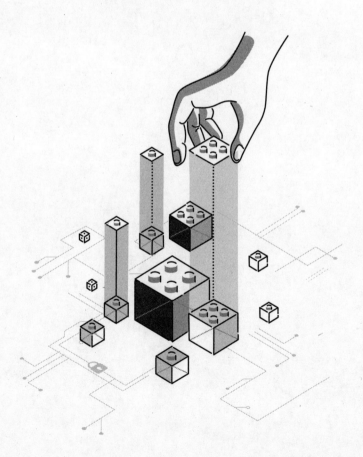

Design Principles

'Design is not just what it looks like and feels like. Design is how it works.'

— Steve Jobs

Policymakers use laws and regulations to achieve policy objectives. Through rules, they spell out exactly how regulated entities must act and stipulate the sanctions that will apply if they do not.

But this approach has its drawbacks. Non-compliance can only be detected after the fact and that too only if there are strong institutional arrangements in place to detect, enforce and adjudicate violations of the law. What's more, because laws have to be expressed in words, no matter how carefully they are drafted, there is always room for interpretation. This ambiguity is further exacerbated when old laws have to deal with new technologies that were not even within the imagination of the draftsmen when the law was enacted.

India's various DPI have been built on a set of common design principles that underpin their functioning. It is how they remain internally consistent and interoperable and why services provided by one digital ecosystem can, with little technical effort, be efficiently consumed and incorporated into another. While these design principles were developed to implement certain technical features, they offer regulators an interesting alternative to the traditional ways in which regulation is done. If deployed carefully, these principles can be more effective than explicitly written laws since they are directly incorporated into the architecture, imposing compliance on all those who wish to use the infrastructure.

In order to explain how this works, let us examine four of the design principles that underpin India's DPI and how they can be used for governance.

Unbundling

Indian DPIs are not mere digitizations of traditional workflows. The architects of India's DPI learnt early that it is only by disassembling workflows into their constituent elements that they can be reassembled into a digital infrastructure that is both resilient and interoperable. This process of taking apart a process to put it back in new and interesting ways is referred to as unbundling. It is how most of India's DPIs have been built and is often why they are successful.

So how does it work?

Operational Workflows

Most operational workflows are made up of a series of steps that need to be followed to go from the first step to the final outcome. If you want to pay someone by cheque, you need a cheque leaf from your bank (YourBank). You then need to fill in the name of the person you are paying and the amount you want to transfer, sign it (ensuring that your signature matches the one on file with your bank) and hand it over to them.

To credit this amount into their bank account, the payee needs to present your cheque to her bank (HerBank), which, in turn, will present it to YourBank for clearance. If banks did this one cheque at a time, it would be terribly inefficient. So in practice, they simply add your cheque to a large pile of cheques that other customers have submitted representing different amounts of money that YourBank is obliged to transfer to HerBank. At the same time, YourBank is accumulating a

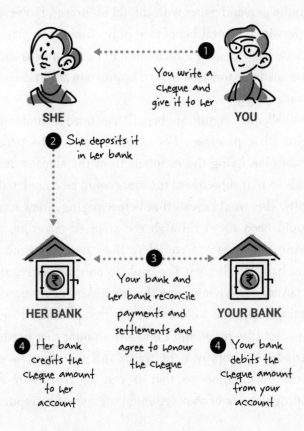

SHE **YOU**

1 You write a cheque and give it to her

2 She deposits it in her bank

HER BANK **YOUR BANK**

3 Your bank and her bank reconcile payments and settlements and agree to honour the cheque

4 Her bank credits the cheque amount to her account

4 Your bank debits the cheque amount from your account

similar list of cheques that its customers have presented them representing the amounts that HerBank needs to pay YourBank. These amounts are reconciled and the balance is transferred to one or the other bank.

Once all this is done, YourBank reduces the balance in your account by the amount that corresponds to the value of the cheque, while HerBank will increase the balance in her bank account by the same amount.

This is a long and somewhat cumbersome process. Depending on the banks involved, it could take days. One way to improve efficiency would be to digitize the processes, to replace the steps that require pen and paper with digital interfaces. However, this only offers incremental benefits – only eliminating errors that might arise from sharing information in non-standard and non-machine-readable formats. It is an improvement but does not go nearly far enough.

To unlock more significant benefits, we need to fundamentally reimagine these processes. For instance, we could separate the process of identifying the recipient from the actual transfer of the funds so that subsequent transfers could be completed more efficiently. This would mean that before paying a new recipient, you would need to go through the steps of recording all the information necessary to complete the payment (name of the recipient bank, the branch, the bank account number and name of the payee) but having done that once, you never need to do that again. Each time you want to pay that person, all you need to do is select the payee and input the amount that needs to be transferred. This improves the traditional workflow by storing transferee information so that it can be repeatedly reused, eliminating the risk of transaction failure caused by input errors.

Unbundling Payments

But we could go even further. So far, we have only been thinking about unbundling the traditional cheque payment workflow. What if we think more ambitiously and try and figure out how to reimagine person-to-person (P2P) payments?

The ultimate P2P payment is cash. It is the most straightforward workflow – all you need to do is take the required amount of cash from your wallet and hand it over to the recipient. You don't need to know who they are, what their bank account is, or any of the other information necessary to make a bank-to-bank transfer (either by cheque or through a digital portal). Is it possible to redesign digital payments to function with the same level of efficiency?

The Indian approach to solving this problem was to insert a new intermediary entity into the payment workflow, the third-party application provider (TPAP). To understand how this works, let us look at a typical digital payment workflow in India from the initial signup with the TPAP to the completion of an actual digital transaction.

Almost all bank accounts in India are linked to a corresponding mobile phone number. When you initially sign up as a new user with a TPAP (Google Pay, PhonePe, BHIM, or any one of the hundreds of applications created by banks and other financial service providers), the TPAP app will request permission to access the banks linked to the mobile number of the device on which it is installed. You can then choose the accounts you want to connect to the TPAP (most of us have a particular account we have set aside for digital payments). The actual linkage of the bank account to the TPAP is carried out by the bank (since it is the only entity authorized to interact with the UPI switch), but TPAP applications have been designed to ensure all this activity takes place behind the scenes so seamlessly that they are invisible to the user.

In order to use your bank account for digital payments, it must first be associated with a virtual payment address (VPA). Think of this as a new digital identity for your bank account, a proxy for all the details that uniquely identify your account and set it up to receive a digital payment. The system has been designed so that VPAs can be freely shared without conveying any confidential information about who you are, where you bank or any of your bank account details.

All digital payments made through this system reference the VPAs of the sender and recipient, and nothing more. Once you have the recipient's VPA, all you need to do is instruct your TPAP app to transfer money from your VPA to that VPA. The transfer takes place in seconds, and both your account and the recipient's are updated instantly.

What is happening behind the scenes is that the moment you initiate the transfer, your TPAP instructs the banks associated with both your VPA and the recipient's VPA to complete the transfer as described. While all customer-facing interactions take place through the interface offered by the TPAP, the mapping of VPAs to bank accounts as well as the actual transfer of funds from payer to payee, all take place within the regulated banking sector.

The National Payments Corporation of India (NPCI) operates the central switch through which all payment transactions are routed for settlement (see the diagram below). While it might appear, from this architecture, that information is progressively concentrated the further up the chain you go, in actual fact, the system is designed to be optimally ignorant. Each entity in the chain is privy to only as much information as is necessary to perform the assigned role.

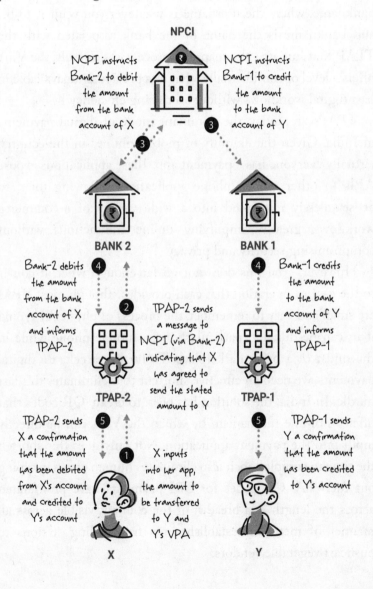

There are several customer-oriented features implicit in the design of this payments ecosystem. In the first place, the VPA gives users an easy-to-remember banking identity that can be shared without risk. This typically takes the form of username@ bankname, where the username is whatever you want it to be, and bankname is the name of the bank associated with the TPAP that initiated the mapping process. As a result, the VPA offers a level of confidentiality that was previously unavailable in past digital workflows without sacrificing efficiency.

TPAPs are, today, the dominant mode of digital payments in India. Given the ubiquity of mobile phones in the country, virtually everyone has a payment app. These applications expose APIs to other mobile phone applications, allowing them to be seamlessly integrated into a wide variety of e-commerce workflows, greatly simplifying online transactions without compromising security and privacy.

However, even this does not go far enough when it comes to the ease of operation that cash provides. Though most VPAs are small and easy to remember, the process of physically typing it in can be difficult, particularly on a mobile phone while in the midst of a busy marketplace. To further accelerate digital payments, we need an effective shortcut that eliminates this last hurdle. In India, the solution has been to create QR codes that offer an offline mechanism by which the VPA can be directly input into the payment application. Not only does this shorten the time to completion, it also eliminates human errors in typing out the VPA. QR codes for UPI payments have proliferated across the length and breadth of the country, visible across all manner of merchant establishments from filling stations to pushcart vegetable vendors.

India unbundled the payment workflow into two parts, the messaging flow and the money flow. The TPAPs were responsible for managing the messaging flow, required to convey payment instructions in a safe and secure manner. The banks were then responsible for the money flows, required to ensure that once they received payment instructions, they debited and credited, respectively, the accounts of the receiver and payer by the same amount.

As is evident from this discussion, if we can unbundle complex workflows and break them down into their constituent elements, we will be able to unlock new efficiencies. While I have, in this section, used the digital payments workflow to illustrate the concept of unbundling, this approach can be applied to any sector.

It is an approach India has adopted time and again in designing its DPI, breaking down traditional workflows to digitally reassemble them in different ways that offer new reimaginings of existing processes.

Unbundling Governance

Unbundling is much harder than it looks. Humans are path dependent and as a result, so reluctant to deviate from the tried and tested workflows that they are often incapable of even imagining that an alternative route can exist. Attempts at unbundling often come up against strong opposition, with naysayers pointing out all the ways in which it will not work. In most instances, these arguments boil down to the view that we should not fix that which is not broken – that it is better to leave things the way they have always been because it is impossible to predict what could happen if we tinker and change things.

But India has proved that unbundling can and does work. In sector after sector, this approach has yielded new workflows that have been deployed with transformative results. After the initial adjustment phase, when users get accustomed to a new way of working, almost all these digital systems have improved efficiency and resulted in greater inclusivity.

This led me to a rather audacious thought – can we unbundle governance?

From one perspective, it is almost imperative to ask this question at this point in time. Having already unbundled workflows across many different sectors, existing contractual and regulatory frameworks are unlikely to continue to remain relevant. Once we change the way the transaction works, we almost have to reimagine the regulations that govern it. Even more importantly, we should use this opportunity to rethink our approach to governance. If we are designing new ways of working, should we not also rebuild our regulatory and contractual methodologies so that our compliance and liability frameworks align more closely with the systems we are redesigning?

Let us first take a look at what the contracts governing these workflows look like. Since DPI establishes relationships between multiple parties, there are essentially two ways in which to think about regulating the rights and obligations of the involved parties.

The first is to craft a single multipartite contract that every party in the ecosystem has to execute and list each of their respective rights and obligations. In a complex ecosystem with multiple different roles and obligations, this would be an extremely complex agreement. The alternative would be to have each party bilaterally execute an agreement with every other participant, setting out their inter se rights and obligations in that document.

The trouble is that, unlike the traditional commercial workflow, India's digital ecosystem allows for the dynamic of constantly shifting sets of parties. As a result, a given transaction could have a completely different cast of characters from every other. To be robust and sustainable, the governance framework needs to take this variance into account.

Take consented data transfers, for example. You could use any one of a number of different consent managers to authorize the transfer of information from the data sources you select to any entity seeking that information. This makes it impractical to design individual contracts between each of the parties.

When we started to reconceptualize this idea in the context of the Open Credit Enablement Network (OCEN) system, we realized that a brand-new contractual framework needed to be designed for the ecosystem approach. Rather than having individual entities sign up for all their roles and responsibilities, there had to be an ecosystem participation agreement that described the obligations of every participant based on the roles they performed. This allowed us to avoid a web of contracts that would have been hard to maintain as the system scaled, giving us, instead, a single agreement that operates as the fulcrum of the ecosystem, and all participants have to accept this. This resulted in everyone becoming contractually bound to everyone else and obliged to carry out the commitments described by the role or roles they agreed to perform.

To do this, we first had to unbundle the *entities* signing up to the contract from the *roles* they performed. This allowed us to attach obligations to what individual parties did rather than who they were. Parties performing multiple roles within the ecosystem were free to indicate all their roles so that they could be bound by the obligations related to each of those roles.

But it was possible to go even further. If our innovation so far was to reimagine the *organization* of the contract, what if we could also reimagine the *content?*

In the process of creating these new digital workflows, it became obvious that many of the contractual obligations of the parties were actually being automatically performed by the code of the digital infrastructure. But even though the system reliably performed these obligations, the parties were still being held contractually liable for its performance. This seemed, at least to me, like an unnecessary redundancy. If the digital ecosystem was designed to perform these tasks, what purpose is served by holding contracting entities liable for actions outside their power?

To be clear, we could have simply ignored this. Standard contractual clauses give lawyers the sort of warm fuzzy feeling that everyone else gets from a pair of well-worn shoes, and it would cost us nothing to retain those clauses even if the very design of the infrastructure ensured the clauses would never be invoked. Having all the provisions a traditional banking lawyer would have expected to see in the contract would certainly have made negotiations less intense.

But not only was this inefficient, it was an inaccurate representation of what would happen if the obligation was not performed. So I sat down with the OCEN team to understand exactly how the technical workflows they had built could be mapped to the contractual obligations we were describing in the ecosystem participation terms. We then removed all the obligations being automatically performed by the system without human intervention from the contractual terms.

When we set out to negotiate these revised terms with the participants of the ecosystem, there was considerable opposition to signing it without the obligations they believed were standard. They were not convinced that those obligations were being performed by the code. What if the code didn't work, they asked. How can we be sure it will work as advertised? If we cannot be sure, we need to include the standard contractual clauses as belts and braces.

It soon became clear that we needed to shift the focus of the negotiations from apportioning liability amongst the parties to assuring them that the code performed as promised. That instead of relying on the contract to enforce their rights, parties needed to assure themselves that the code worked as advertised. Instead of having lawyers negotiating liability and the consequences of their inter se obligations, we needed to get engineers to test the code to assure the organization that it performed as it was supposed to. If they had that assurance, they didn't need to get that comfort from the terms of the contract.

I must hasten to add that this approach – of implementing contractual obligations through code – is not new. The cryptocurrency ecosystems – and in particular those of the more advanced blockchain ecosystems like Ethereum and Polygon – already offer smart contract functionalities, allowing obligations to be encoded and contracts to be self-executing. The trouble is that to take advantage of these features, participants need to commit fully to the crypto ecosystem. This means designing the operational frameworks around the token-based architecture that characterizes the governance of these ecosystems. In most regulated sectors, this would simply not be feasible. Since the DPI approach creates new digital ecosystems within which a number of contractual obligations can be executed, it should be possible to implement the smart contract features that were touted as a core promise of the crypto ecosystem. And with the DPI approach extending to more and more sectors, it should, in time, be possible to cover a wider canvas.

Lessons Learnt from Unbundling

There are two lessons we can learn from the unbundling design principle that can apply broadly to the governance of DPI.

First, just as it is possible to take apart operational workflows, breaking them down into constituent parts, it is possible to disassemble traditional contractual arrangements into fundamental elements. When we do this, we may realize how different elements of the governance architecture can be reassembled in new and interesting ways that are often far better suited for the new digital architectures they are describing. Instead of force-fitting new digital workflows into traditional contractual structures, it is more efficient to reimagine how these contracts are constructed.

Second, since digital workflows automatically perform the obligations that used to be performed manually, a trusted and well-tested digital infrastructure can reassure parties that these obligations will be performed reliably, time and again, across a large number of transactions. This will allow us to pare down and reshape contracts, removing clauses referring to the obligations performed automatically by code, making the terms of participation in this digital ecosystem simpler and easier to implement.

This insight can also apply to legislators. Rather than force-fitting new digital ecosystems into existing regulatory constructs, they should design regulatory frameworks to be more naturally suited to regulating these new ecosystems. In doing so, they should identify afresh the harms that may result from these new frameworks and establish regulatory safeguards to mitigate these risks to the greatest extent possible. At the same time, they should keep an eye on the positive outcomes that can be achieved and ensure they include appropriate incentives to that end.

Unbundling is not so much a feature of the system as an approach to how it is designed. As a result, the discussion in this section, so far, has been about how governance should be reimagined. All the other design principles in this chapter describe features of India's DPIs and the unique benefits and efficiencies that they offer. I believe that if we truly understand what these core design elements are, we can achieve governance outcomes in new, more efficient ways. This is central to understanding how a techno-legal governance framework should be designed.

Interoperability

When we say Aadhaar is a digital identity, most people believe this refers to the fact that the process it uses to establish identity is fundamentally digital. They relate immediately to the biometric scanners used for enrolment and deduplication and the authentication processes that compare identity information against the Central Identities Data Repository.

But this is only half the story. Aadhaar is arguably the first national identity system designed to be directly incorporated into digital workflows through publicly accessible application programming interfaces (APIs). As a result, the authentication and KYC features that it offers could be leveraged by several different services that simply use these APIs to confirm that a given Aadhaar number corresponds to a named individual and the demographic information related to that person.

Interoperating with Aadhaar

The fact that it is digital and interoperable has made it possible to use Aadhaar in novel ways, many of which may not even have been imagined by those involved in its design. One such example is Jeevan Praman, a government pension service that uses Aadhaar authentication to remotely establish whether or not a pensioner is actually alive when their pension is due.

In the rural hinterland, the only way for retirees to collect their pension was by showing up in person before the officer responsible for payments to demonstrate that they were still alive and, therefore, eligible for their pension. Given the remoteness of so many Indian villages, this often meant that old people had to travel great distances in order to get paid.

Jeevan Praman leverages the 'liveness' guarantee implicit in biometric authentication to eliminate this requirement. Now pensioners simply have to present themselves before any Aadhaar authentication agency in their village and prove that they are still alive by offering their biometrics for authentication. Once this confirmation has been received, the pension is automatically transferred to them.

Interoperability enables the cross-pollination of services which, in turn, leads to diversity of innovation and efficiency of design. When DPIs are designed to function as discrete, sufficiently isolated building blocks, they can either stand on their own, performing the specific, unbundled workflows they were designed to perform, or they can be used in combination with other digital building blocks to contribute to a range of complex multistep workflows.

If all of India's digital infrastructure is internally consistent, it is not because every last element of the infrastructure was conceptualized before the first element was even built. Instead, it is because they were all designed to be extensible and interoperable. As a result, not only can different elements of India's DPI connect to other existing DPIs, they can also connect to DPIs that haven't yet been built. This means that a new DPI can be built on existing digital infrastructure without reinventing the wheel each time.

This is of particular importance when building DPI at population-scale in a country as large as India. It is far more efficient to incorporate widely used digital building blocks into subsequent layers of the stack instead of having to replicate them each time from scratch. Where a DPI already exists to uniquely identify individual users, it is more efficient to use it as the authentication module for a new digital infrastructure than to build this functionality afresh. When a digital ecosystem is looking to offer the payment functionality to its users, it is far more efficient to integrate existing payment infrastructure into it than to build it from scratch.

Interoperable digital infrastructure is more efficient and internally consistent. Digital building blocks can be reused by other systems to allow designers to focus on new challenges while relying on existing building blocks to perform the necessary functions. Where these digital systems require data contained in other systems, they can be assured that this data will be available with no loss in fidelity as long as the two systems are interoperable – all of which is essential for scale.

What may not be immediately apparent is what bearing any of this has on governance.

Interoperable Governance

Every piece of code contains within it a set of constraints that describe how it can be used. These could relate to how the data is collected or the uses to which it is put. The decision to ensure that a piece of code performs in a specific way often reflects a specific governance philosophy, even though the developers might not have thought of it in those terms. Regardless, that philosophy suffuses the entire digital system, preventing any behaviours that do not align with it.

When a piece of code is designed to be extensible and interoperable, the rules embedded into it will similarly extend to every other digital system it is connected to. Where these rules reflect a specific governance philosophy, that philosophy will automatically apply to all the other systems that depend on it. In other words, the governance philosophy encoded into interoperable DPI can be extended to every other DPI that depends on it.

For example, take Aadhaar authentication. There were many ways in which these features could have been implemented. For instance, authenticating officials could have been allowed to search the identity database for information about a person to authenticate them. While this might have been a more efficient solution for the authenticator, giving third parties the right to search the database would have meant that they would have been be able to access not only a specific individual's information but also anyone else in the national database they cared to search for. This, from a privacy perspective, was far from optimal. Instead, Aadhaar has implemented a far more conservative approach by only offering a 'yes–no' answer to any authentication request. This design choice – to adopt a privacy-oriented approach over a more convenient search facility – is now a core feature of the Aadhaar system.

Any other digital public infrastructure that wants to use Aadhaar authentication as part of its workflow has no alternative but to incorporate this 'yes–no' authentication. It doesn't matter that for their particular use case, it would have been far more useful to be able to search the Aadhaar database. This is all that the system permits one to do and every interoperating system needs to work within that constraint. As a result, the privacy features built into the design of Aadhaar can be extended to every other infrastructure connected to it.

It is possible to imagine how design choices might apply in several different circumstances. If a given DPI is built to allow data to be transferred only if it has received the electronic consent of the person to whom that data pertains, every other digital infrastructure that uses that DPI to receive data is obliged to adhere to that consent requirement. Similarly, where a DPI is designed so that the data contained in it automatically expires after a stipulated time or immediately after it has been used, all other DPI that have connected to it in order to access that data are subject to the same data retention restrictions.

This is granular governance – the ability to embed a particular governance philosophy into an elemental building block of the DPI ecosystem and have it influence every other DPI to which it is connected. This gives regulators and legislators the tools they can use to carefully craft techno-legal governance frameworks to achieve specific regulatory outcomes. Where privacy can be embedded into the design of an interoperable digital building block, we no longer have to worry about separately engineering it into every new DPI that we create. All we need to do is ensure that we interoperate with that block.

Federation

Another feature of the design of Indian DPI is that it leaves data where it was collected in different pools at the far edges of the digital ecosystem instead of aggregated in the centre into a single data lake. This conscious decision to federate the storage of data instead of centralizing it offers specific governance benefits to the design of the overall architecture. To understand this, we first need to understand the underlying incentives that brought us to this point.

One of the challenges of working with data is access. Data resides in proprietary silos that are inaccessible – even by those to whom that data pertains. This means that even if I know that a data fiduciary has some data that pertains to me, there is no effective way for me to access that data so I can share it with someone else. Because data is so hard to access, it is collected afresh each time a new business needs to use it to provide services to its customer. This results in the creation of yet another data silo that is just as hard to access and compounds the problem instead of solving it.

Take, for example, the medical information you generate each time you visit a doctor or hospital. Most hospitals have proprietary systems that collect and store test results and medical diagnoses so that they can be easily retrieved the next time you visit. Given how important some of this information can be in an emergency (say, data about any drugs you might be allergic to and the medications you are currently on), there is a legitimate interest in the hospital retaining this information. However, there are times when you might want a second opinion – another point of view from a doctor in some other hospital. Unfortunately, as good as hospital systems are at storing your information, it is notoriously difficult to extract this data from it – even if it is yours to begin with. As a result, more often than not, you end up repeating all those tests every time you go elsewhere for a second opinion. The more doctors you consult, the greater the number of different and unconnected silos you end up creating.

This phenomenon repeats itself across several different domains – from financial services to the sharing economy. Not only is this inefficient, it is highly wasteful of our resources. The world is in search of an alternative.

One way to address this problem might have been to design a system that collects all the data pertaining to a given individual from the various silos in which they were stored, aggregating them into a single central repository placed under the control of the data principal. Tim Berners-Lee's Solid project attempts just that, creating 'pods' of data under the users' control. Personal data can be stored in these pods and shared subject to conditions of use that are prescribed through code by the pod.

While this might bring data under the control of the user,

it does so by replacing one type of data silo with another – one that is under the control of the user. As much as this may assure the user that they have a greater degree of autonomy over what is done with their data, it shifts the responsibility of ensuring the safety and security of that data from the data fiduciary to the data principal. Aggregating all the data pertaining to a given individual in one place, potentially creates a honey pot for malicious hackers who previously would have had to break into multiple different data servers to access the information that has now been neatly organized for them in a single place.

Connecting Data Silos

Another way to solve the problem of access would be to establish a data transfer infrastructure that reliably allows data to be accessed as and when it is needed. This is what India has attempted to do through its DEPA architecture. It has made it possible for different data silos to access each other using a common digital infrastructure through which data can be made to flow under the authority and with the consent of the data principal. This means that data remains where it was collected, but with the consent of the person to whom it pertains, it can be moved to some other entity. Instead of requiring data principals to accumulate their data at a central location, they can just access it whenever they need to.

DEPA is one example of how India's DPI is designed, leaving data at source instead of aggregating it into one central location. While the DEPA approach relies on permissioned access, other workflows tokenize the data at source so that all subsequent operations carried out using that data do not expose the underlying personal data of the individual. This is how UPI has been designed – mapping all the bank information required to complete a digital payment to a virtual payment address (VPA) which is all that is shared to receive payments. The VPA is thus just a token that represents important personal information of the user using a non-identifiable proxy.

Similarly, Aadhaar has been designed to ensure that the only access to identity information is provided through an authentication interface that can only return a yes–no answer in response to an authentication query. This ensures that individuals can be reliably identified without having to accumulate personal information in the hands of the authenticator. While Aadhaar's eKYC interface can provide additional demographic information to the authenticator, its use is subject to more constraints than yes–no authentication – to the point where even those who are permitted to carry out eKYC do not have access to core biometric information.

But my favourite example of how the philosophy of data federation has been implemented in the DPI ecosystem is DigiYatra – a service that enables paperless access into Indian airports from kerbside entry points all the way to the boarding gate. DigiYatra has been specifically designed to ensure that all personal data is securely stored in a digital wallet within the DigiYatra app on the user's phone. Shortly before the scheduled time of departure, that information is associated with the relevant travel information and shared with the airport so that the passenger can pass through all the relevant checkpoints. No later than 24 hours after the departure of the flight, that information is purged from all airport systems. The biometric image of the user and the associated identity information remains on the phone at all times.

By letting data remain where it was collected, data fiduciaries continue to retain control over the data that they spent time and resources collecting. At the same time, building infrastructure that connects these federated data stores so as to permit this data to be transferred with the user's consent restores to the user a level of autonomy over the data. By enabling data principals to access data under the control of data fiduciaries, they can share it with other service providers, in turn reducing the latter's incentive to collect it once again and creating yet another inaccessible data silo. This allows the benefits of data to be dispersed more widely, increasing its use in the ecosystem. It also ensures that personal data does not unnecessarily proliferate through the system by using tokens to serve as a digital representation of the personal data without disclosing any of the personal information implicit in it.

How Federation Improves Governance

These examples of how Indian DPI implements data storage serve to illustrate the sundry governance benefits of adopting a federated approach.

As much as DEPA is primarily a data protection framework, its federated design demonstrates how technology infrastructures can offer a new alternative to how we have traditionally thought about dealing with data monopolies. Big tech companies that, through the careful accumulation of customer data, have established powerful data monopolies prevent competition from new entrants with the help of the data moats they have established. This has a chilling effect on innovation since no one can even dream of coming up with a competing product without access to data. DEPA offers a solution to that problem by describing how data contained in silos can, under the instructions of the data principal, be shared with other service providers. This not only returns autonomy to the user, it also ensures that the benefits of data can more equitably be used through the ecosystem – which is particularly important in a developing country context.

In UPI, the personal financial information of a given user is associated with a non-identifiable token which ensures that, from that point onwards, the user is effectively anonymous in all transactions in the workflow. By tokenizing sensitive personal information in this manner, operational information necessary for completing the workflow can be left at source (where it was created) without any appreciable impact on the efficiency of the transaction workflows. This achieves the governance outcomes of ensuring greater personal privacy without affecting the efficiency of the digital workflow.

The decision to build Aadhaar authentication so that it does not disclose demographic information on an authentication request but merely indicates whether the Aadhaar number corresponds to the name of the individual ensures that no personal data leaves the identity database other than that which has already been provided to the authenticator by the user. By limiting the data that is accessible through the authentication framework, it programmatically ensures that only a minimal amount of information is accessible, leaving the rest within the database.

DigiYatra ensures that personal data remains, as far as possible, in the mobile phone of the user, ensuring that highly sensitive biometric information remains in the direct physical control of the user at all times so that the sensitive personal information always remains under the control of the user.

Designing digital infrastructure to optimize this federated approach to data offers governance benefits that address some of the key challenges of competition, data protection and security. When federation is built directly into the architecture of the system, it ensures that the mere act of using digital public infrastructure ensures compliance with regulatory obligations.

Protocols

Much of India's digital infrastructure has been explicitly designed as a protocol and not a platform. What this means is that rather than building out a platform to deliver the services that a given digital application is supposed to provide, Indian regulators have simply described the protocols to which market participants must conform and invited the private sector to build out the infrastructure based on these protocols. This allows the ecosystem to benefit from the sort of innovation that only the private sector can bring while at the same time making sure that it conforms to the constraints imposed by the protocol.

Since any eligible private sector entity is eligible to participate and is free to design its own applications as it sees fit, so long as it adheres to the basic protocol that has been specified, the resulting ecosystem remains coherent while still allowing competitive innovation to flourish. Market pressures ensure that all participants in the ecosystem keep their offerings current, knowing that a failure to do so will result in their competitors stealing a march over them in the market. This fosters a sense of healthy competition, with various market participants vying to outdo each other with newer and better features. This, in turn, benefits data principals who get to use products that are constantly improving thanks to this competitive market-driven innovation.

Protocols Not Platforms

While the foundational element of IndiaStack – Aadhaar – was entirely built and continues to be operated by the government, every subsequent layer has been built with progressively greater and greater levels of private sector participation. In all sectors, however, the core protocols remain under the control of the government and the applicable sector regulators.

The Unified Payment Interface (UPI) protocol was published by India's central bank – the Reserve Bank of India – and is managed and supervised by Reserve Bank Information Technology Private Limited, a wholly-owned subsidiary of Reserve Bank that was set up to serve its IT and cybersecurity needs. Private sector companies have designed applications to conform to these protocols and to provide an interface for consumers (through mobile applications that they develop, manage and operate) that are used to access the payment infrastructure. The payment system works because every consumer-facing application conforms to the same protocols and those operate as the connective tissue between the banking systems that they need to interconnect with to make the entire ecosystem work.

DEPA, the most advanced layer of the stack, is also just a protocol designed to connect different sets of private enterprises to each other through intermediate consent manager entities. The connection between the consent manager and the tech systems of these data fiduciaries is only possible because the latter have themselves, in their role as information providers in the DEPA ecosystem, conformed their systems to the DEPA protocols that apply to data fiduciaries. This ensures that no matter how the underlying system has been designed, the way it interoperates with the participants in the DEPA ecosystem is as specified in the protocol.

Though this might not be obvious at first glance, none of India's DPI are platforms. While our interactions with them take place through mobile applications and websites that make it seem like we are engaging on a platform, they are all applications connected to each other over a common protocol. This offers regulators new and interesting opportunities to exert their authority.

Regulating Through Protocols

In the case of most of India's DPI, control over the protocol vests with the regulator, who therefore has the power to determine exactly how the ecosystem will function. All it needs to do to alter the manner in which it operates is to implement a subtle change to the protocol. Since all market participants need to update their systems to reflect these protocol changes if they wish to continue to use the ecosystem, any modification of the protocol has the effect of instantaneously rewriting the rules of the game.

From a regulators' perspective, this means that regulatory and policy objectives can be achieved by just selectively altering the protocol. Unlike traditional regulatory measures, whose effects often lag significantly behind the legal instruments through which they are brought to life, changes to the protocol have an immediate effect. This is a far more effective means of enforcing regulatory compliance than anything else that currently exists.

Having said that, protocols only describe the base requirements that need to be fulfilled in order for one element of the infrastructure to interact effectively with the others. While they do prescribe the guardrails, they leave room for innovation on all aspects not specifically addressed by the protocol. So long as the application conforms to the basic protocol, developers are free to innovate howsoever they choose. As a result, while protocols ensure minimal levels of conformity between different elements of the infrastructure, they enable innovation, thereby allowing users to benefit from competition.

Regulators who appreciate how protocols can be used to achieve regulatory objectives will find it to be a powerful tool. For instance, if a few private sector players have begun to dominate participation in a given DPI sector and reduced competition in that space, the regulator should be able to tweak the protocol by introducing rate limiters that compel the participants to share transactions more equitably around the ecosystem. This will require regulators to not only carefully monitor the market, detecting failures before they become too big to reverse, but also to assess the market outcomes that any adjustment of the protocol could have. Regulators must ensure that none of the interventions they make end up having a detrimental effect on innovation within the ecosystem. Protocols that have been defined too narrowly will end up stifling the ecosystem. On the other hand, unless they impose sufficient restraint on market players, they will not be able to mitigate against the harmful consequences of aggressive innovation.

This sort of approach is far in excess of what regulators

currently do. If they are to take advantage of these new governance tools, they will need to establish new institutional frameworks to augment their current capabilities. This should include monitoring arrangements designed to detect market failures well before they occur, as well as technical design capabilities to ensure that tweaks in the protocol are administered appropriately. Since regulators rarely have these capabilities, the industry will need to establish institutional arrangements to fill these gaps. This could take the form of self-regulatory organizations that operate within specific sectors as well as technical standards organizations that specialize in designing the protocols based upon which these ecosystems operate.

The design principles mentioned in this chapter are merely illustrative. Almost all discussions of India's DPI describe a much broader range of features, all of which can, in the hands of a sufficiently creative regulator, be adapted to achieve various regulatory outcomes. But these solutions tend to be more subtle, operating at the level of the infrastructure layer.

It is possible to take the regulatory design even further. To incorporate elements of the legal code directly into the software code that consumers and market participants use to interact with each other. It is possible to embed code in code.

Techno-Legal Governance

'The best way to predict the future is to invent it.'

– Alan Kay

The first time I read Code and the Other Laws of Cyberspace by Laurence Lessig was over twenty years ago. I was a young lawyer at the time, and the book was, to me, a masterclass on how to break down complex legal and technical issues so that they could be understood by a lay audience. In the years since, I have pretty much built my career around trying to take a similar approach to thinking about how technology should be regulated – both in my writing as well as the policy work that I have been engaged with.

In his book, Lessig opined that the internet is regulated by four forces – laws, norms, markets and code. Of these, code, he argued, was the most powerful, given its ability to directly shape online behaviour and values. He was particularly concerned about the implications of this, realizing that if misused, code could undermine democracy, privacy and freedom on the internet. Rereading his book twenty years later, it is remarkable how prescient his insights were. So many of the challenges we are dealing with today might have been nipped in the bud had we taken heed of his warnings.

Modern digital ecosystems have been built by private enterprises. They created the all-pervasive digital ecosystems that are ubiquitous today, along with the many digital services that are now indispensable to our daily lives. But precisely because we left it to private companies to determine what behaviour the code would shape and how, many of Lessig's fears have come to pass.

In most instances, the sole incentive of the enterprises that built the modern internet was commercial gain. The code they wrote responded directly to those imperatives. Where the revenue model of the business was advertising, the digital infrastructure it built was optimized to collect information about users so that advertisements could be more accurately targeted at them. Where the objective of the digital system was to improve the efficiency of the administrative departments of a hospital or other healthcare establishment, the business optimized for billing efficiencies over ensuring that health data is processed in a manner that is useful to doctors and medical staff.

As a result, the behaviours that code shapes lead to unfavourable outcomes. Social media ecosystems where code was designed to target advertising at users most likely to consume them were easily subverted to deliver false information to those most likely to believe it was true. Hospital information management systems that have been designed to serve the needs of the billing department and insurance companies are virtually useless for doctors and medical staff who need the data contained in them to treat patients.

This has resulted in a culture of data aggregation. As

businesses began to realize that the value of data increases with concentration, they did all they could to collect more and more of it, locking it up in large inaccessible data silos for future, as yet unnamed, even unthought-of purposes. Apart from unleashing a twisted competition between data businesses to amass increasingly large amounts of information, the aggregation removed personal data from the control of those it pertained to, preventing data principals from reaping the benefits that could otherwise have accrued to them.

Legislators around the world have tried to address these concerns by enacting laws that prescribe how technology businesses ought to function. For the most part, these regulations try and break the stranglehold that large incumbent data companies have over data so that it can be more equitably used in ways that will both promote competition and achieve outcomes that benefit the data principals to whom they pertain. These efforts have had negligible results.

As we have seen, most of the behaviours they are looking to prohibit have already been hardwired into the underlying technologies on which these companies have built. The changes regulators seek to enforce run contrary to the incentives which drive the business models that collect and hoard data by design.

As a result, the companies to whom these laws apply look to comply with only that much of the law as is strictly necessary. At every step, they design their business to skirt around the very edge of what is required for compliance with regulations, constantly pushing against the letter of the law with aggressive interpretations that preserve as much of their existing business model as possible. Despite increasingly aggressive attempts at enforcement, not much has changed in this regard.

We need to borrow a leaf out of Lawrence Lessig's book. Where so much of our lives is driven by technology, we can no longer just rely on laws to regulate code. Instead, we need to embed, directly into the technology infrastructure upon which modern society operates, the democratic principles that legislators are trying to enforce through statute. We can hope to hold the rapacious data-gathering practices of private technology companies in check only when the underlying code itself conforms to the principles according to which society must be governed. Given how deeply private digital infrastructure is entrenched, this is a daunting task.

The problem is figuring out how to redesign our existing technology systems to comply with these principles. Across all sectors of the economy – from health, financial services and education to commerce and the law – private technology systems are deeply entrenched and shape how our world is organized. Getting these systems to adapt and change is akin to moving mountains.

Instead of redesigning the way in which existing systems have been designed, we can instead build new technology infrastructures that connect different data systems to each other. In this way, could we not allow the data contained within these systems to become more accessible while ensuring more privacy and security? By giving those to whom this data pertains easier access to their own information, such a system will be able to make that data available to other data businesses, who could then provide a wider and more efficiently organized range of services.

This is what India has attempted to do with DEPA – the technology infrastructure that enables the transfer of data from one data business to another with the consent of the person to whom that data pertains. In an earlier chapter, we discussed how DEPA works and the many benefits that it brings to those who need to leverage their own data as information collateral. We demonstrated how it implements the transfer of data using a consent-based workflow that allows the data principal to determine what can or cannot be done with their data using completely digital workflows.

What we did not discuss is how DEPA incorporates into its design legal principles that are otherwise only found in statutes. And how, to that extent, it is a technological framework that implements, through the design of its architecture, legal obligations that are otherwise only expressed in statutes. This is a new techno-legal approach to data governance that can, I believe, be successfully applied across several different areas of governance.

But in order to understand how, we first need to understand how DEPA does this.

Privacy

As discussed previously, most data protection regulations are centred around a set of common principles universally regarded as assuring an acceptable level of data protection. I had organized them for convenience under three broad categories: (i) those that ensure user autonomy over their data, (ii) those that protect against disproportionate access and (iii) those that require confidentiality and security of the data.

Let us now examine whether the techno-legal architecture that DEPA describes provides through code what the data protection principles require us to comply with through statute.

Portability

A data principal has autonomy over their data if they have control over what is done with it at various stages in its life cycle. Initially, this control is exercised through the consent they provide for its collection. However, once it passes into the control of the data fiduciary, their effective control over what can or cannot be done with it diminishes significantly or is completely nullified.

Modern data protection regulations look to right this wrong by giving data principals additional rights. All data principals have the right to access and correction that allows them to ask any data fiduciary whether or not they are processing any personal data pertaining to them. If the answer is yes, they can insist on reviewing these data and, where necessary, make amendments to bring it up to date. They can also exert their right to data portability and insist that the data fiduciary transfer (or port) that information to them in an intelligible machine-readable format.

DEPA does pretty much the same thing using a more efficient technology solution than is typically deployed. It puts in place a framework that establishes digital connections between various data silos through a new institutional innovation called the consent manager. In the process, it facilitates the transfer of data in an efficient manner that can actually be used to the benefit of the data principal. This technological framework gives data principals autonomy over their data even when it is under the control of a data fiduciary. It gives them access to data that pertains to them, which would otherwise have remained buried in a data silo far beyond their ability to access.

DEPA is also an implementation of the right to data portability – but the way in which it implements the right is significantly different from the way in which it is traditionally implemented. Most modern data fiduciaries have set up workflows that comply with their portability obligations under modern data protection statutes. Anyone can approach them and demand that all of their personal data, which may be under the control of that data fiduciary, should be identified and transferred to them in a format they can read. Having made such a request myself, for both my Twitter (now 'X') and Facebook data, I can confirm that not only is this possible, the process is, by and large, painless.

That said, having obtained that data, it quickly becomes apparent that there is precious little that can be done with it. While it may have been provided in a machine-readable format, most of us have accumulated such vast amounts of data on these platforms that without an above-average level of technical capability, there is precious little that we can do with it. At best, I can now rest easy knowing that in the unlikely event that either of those stalwarts of the social media industry go bust, my posts, as of the date on which I downloaded them, will still be available to me offline.

DEPA, on the other hand, has been designed to support requests for specific items of data – to cull out a subset of information that responds to a specific request and to only share that specific subset with the designated data fiduciary. This implements a form of data portability that gives data principals more granular control over what can or cannot be done with their data than is possible under other systems.

Why is this useful?

In a world where data has transformed from mere information to information collateral, the availability of specific information can form the basis upon which service providers extend services to you. A verifiable record of financial transactions, for example, could be the basis upon which a fintech company determines whether or not you are eligible for credit.

DEPA makes it possible for data to be shared in this manner, allowing those who need this information to easily access it with the digital consent of the user. Because this entire process is carried out in an end-to-end digital workflow, it dramatically simplifies traditional processes, resulting in savings in cost and time. And since no data can even move without the digitally signed electronic consent of the data principal, it preserves the autonomy of the data principal over the data.

Which brings us to the second feature of the DEPA framework, which ensures that the data principal has autonomy over their data.

Consent

Almost all data protection laws list consent as legitimate grounds for the processing of personal data. To many, it is the primary ground for processing – the mere fact that a data principal has approved the collection or processing of personal data is often seen as a necessary and sufficient proof of the validity of any subsequent processing of that data.

However, traditional implementations of consent are flawed. Since it is easiest to collect consent when the data principal is signing up for a given service for the first time, most data services tend to describe the purposes for which the data will be used in the broadest possible terms by covering a range of purposes so broad as to be all-encompassing. One way to make consent more meaningful would be to ensure that it is so easy to obtain that whenever it needs to be used for a different purpose, the consent to do so can be easily collected afresh.

Under DEPA, the data principal's approval for any transfer of data is provided by using the electronic consent artefact – a protocol that allows anyone seeking such consent to record the *purpose* for which the data is sought to be transferred, *who* it is to be transferred to and the *duration* for which it will be retained. The use of the consent artefact in this manner electronically implements the data protection principles of notice and consent, purpose specification and retention restrictions. Since it is digitally signed, it offers a non-repudiable record of the information that was requested and also of the data principals' consent to provide it.

Since this consent is obtained immediately before the data is collected, the data principal can assess the implications of providing consent far more effectively than would have been the case where consent was provided at the time of signing up for the service for some as-yet-undefined future purpose. Since the entity to which the data is being transferred is clearly specified, the data principal has certainty as to the intended recipient and is not providing consent for the transfer to a broadly defined but not specifically named set of entities.

DEPA implements consent in a digital format where most other frameworks set up privacy policies and upfront consent arrangements in response to the statutory obligation to do so. In DEPA, users' consent is provided through an application on their mobile phones that presents them all the relevant information they need to make a decision in a format that is easy to understand. To those familiar with UPI, the user experience is very similar. Since DEPA makes it so easy to ask and obtain consent we now have the flexibility to reimagine how consent requests should be designed.

We have all grown accustomed to clicking 'I Agree' when we sign up for a new service on our computer or mobile device. What we are doing when we click on that button is agreeing to the terms of service and privacy policy of the website we are about to sign up to. Since the service will reasonably only get one chance to get us to agree to terms and conditions, they end up front-loading a whole lot of terms into this document we agree to when we enrol. If you have ever read through the terms of service of any of the websites you frequently use, you will be struck by how broadly it is framed and the range of different future purposes that have been specified.

This is done deliberately. Since companies believe, and rightly so, that their customers do not want to be bothered with repeated consent requests, they tend to cram as much as possible into the terms of services and privacy policy that users agree to when they sign up for the service. They frame these documents in the broadest possible terms to cover as many current and future use cases that they can think of so that should they decide to use your data for any other purpose, there will be some provision or the other in these agreements that will allow them to do so.

As you will appreciate, the consent granted to do such future acts is less than meaningful. If I agree to allow you to do something way into the future, I have no real appreciation for how that will pan out when you decide to go ahead and do it. My circumstances could have changed – including my relationship with you and anyone else whom these services involve – and I may no longer want you to do those things that I had agreed to way back in the past. However, since I have already allowed you to go ahead and use my data for this purpose, there is little I can do to stop you. This is the problem with consent as it is commonly collected today.

DEPA is designed to allow future transfers to take place based on consent that has been provided proximally to that transfer. As a result, you can evaluate for yourself whether, in fact, you want to share that data just before the transfer actually takes place. By bringing the decision close to the actual transfer itself, DEPA offers data principals greater control over the use of their data.

Forking Consent

In time, once companies realize that they can always turn to DEPA for any of their data transfer needs, they might be willing to pare down the broadly stated transfer rights in their privacy policies so that those documents only cover the immediate, direct uses to which that data will be put. While this could be imposed upon them by regulation, I would prefer this to come about through the operation of market forces.

I would like to think that at least some companies will look to differentiate themselves from their competition on the basis of their privacy practices. These companies can categorically state that data will be collected for only a limited set of uses, relying on consent obtained through DEPA for any future data they might need.

When this happens, I can see consent itself fork into two. When we sign up for a service, we will provide our consent for data to be collected from us so that it can be processed for the purposes of providing the services we signed up to. I like to call this consent 'collection consent' because it authorizes the collection of data for the immediate purposes for which the user signed up. At a later point in time, that data might be required for other purposes – by different service providers from those who initially collected it. They will activate the DEPA framework to initiate a data transfer and, if permitted, will be given access to a portion of the data initially collected. I like to call this consent 'consent to port' because it refers to the permission needed to transfer data at a later point in time – well after it was initially collected.

This bifurcation of consent into *collection consent* and *consent to port* offers greater privacy assurances than that which is currently available.

Disproportionate Access

The autonomy granted to a data principal ensures that no data can be collected or transferred without their consent and that if they want, they can demand that the data about them under the control of a given data fiduciary is transferred to another data fiduciary. However, we know from bitter experience that consent is easily obtained. We are often busy, impatient to get the services we were promised. Instead of carefully reading through the terms of the privacy policy, we simply click 'I Agree', trusting that the party we are contracting with will do us no harm. In the process, we end up agreeing to share more data than is entirely good for us.

If left to the data fiduciary to design, consent can be requested in such broad terms as to give the data fiduciary access to far more information than is strictly necessary. This results in more data being collected and placed in the hands of the fiduciary, exacerbating the lack of control of the data principal over what is being done with their data.

The further and possibly more serious concern has to do with its use. While most data protection statutes clearly stipulate the purpose for which it can be collected and processed, once data has passed into the hands of the data fiduciary, there is precious little the data principal can do to ensure that the data is used for the stipulated purpose. All they can do is hope and pray that it is being used as promised – and for no other purposes.

In both these instances, the data fiduciary is able to gain access to more data than should have been possible and use that data in ways that it ought not. It is able to do so despite the fact that the data principal has been vested with complete autonomy to decide what should or should not be done with that data. Most data protection statutes enact special additional measures to ensure that they mitigate the risk of disproportionate access to data even though they have already put in place measures to ensure autonomy.

The first line of defence against disproportionate data access is the purpose specification clause, which is now a feature of most modern data protection laws. This provision requires data fiduciaries to state the purposes for which data is being collected in terms sufficiently narrow so that they clearly limit the data that can be collected. Stated differently, data fiduciaries are prohibited from framing their consent request in an over-broad manner that gives them access to more data than is strictly necessary for a specific, well-defined purpose.

However, provisions such as these run contrary to the natural incentives according to which data businesses are organized. The more information they have about their customers, the more efficiently services can be targeted at them. As a result, despite the strict stipulation to frame purpose narrowly, businesses do their best to include as wide a swathe of purposes as possible in the consent requests. This, in turn, means that consent regulation becomes a matter of enforcement as it is up to the regulator to keep data fiduciaries from stretching the purposes they specify wider than necessary.

Consent Templates

DEPA enforces purpose specification for data transfers, encoding a purpose field into the consent artefact that is used to process a data transfer request. The system is designed so that it will not process a transfer request if the consent request does not specify a purpose. In addition, further constraints are imposed on what consent can be sought through the use of consent templates.

A data business that wants to use DEPA for the transfer of data has to choose from a set of consent templates to specify the exact type of information that it needs. Keeping in mind the wide variety of potential uses, a range of different templates have been prepared. These templates have been designed with specific use cases in mind, and for each such use case, it will list the specific information requested. Through the use of consent templates, DEPA implements purpose specification by ensuring that participants in the ecosystem do not indiscriminately collect data beyond what is permitted by that template.

At present, DEPA is being actively deployed in the financial services sector in India. Consent templates relate, for the most part, to data that will help assess a borrower's entitlement for a loan based on what information is available from the participants in the ecosystem. As more and more participants with different data sets are added to the ecosystem and as the framework is extended to other sectors, new templates will have to be developed to address the data processing requirements in those domains. It goes without saying that no consent template will permit a participant to transfer all the data under the control of a given data fiduciary.

Consent templates will need to be approved by the regulator. Since it is likely that DEPA will eventually be operational across a number of different sectors, these will need to be developed, in the first instance, by the self-regulatory organizations that operate in a given sector. These organizations will have a finger on the pulse of the ecosystem and a responsibility to ensure that the system as a whole operates in a manner consistent with widely accepted principles of data protection. By implementing purpose specification through code in a manner that augments the statutory obligation that all data fiduciaries are, in any event, required to comply with, DEPA offers a new approach to curb disproportionate data access.

That said, the consent template only provides the means by which the notice provided under the consent artefact is framed appropriately in order to get as much information as is necessary for the stated purpose and no more. What it cannot do is ensure that the data fiduciary receiving that information does not, in actual fact, use it for an entirely different purpose. At best, the consent artefact serves to operate as a record of the terms agreed by the parties – but cannot itself be used to enforce it.

I should hasten to add, at this time, that this is no different from the position we find ourselves in today. Every time we enrol ourselves into a new service, the data fiduciaries who collect information from us list, in their terms of service, the limited purposes for which our data will be used. But beyond this promise, this bald statement in their privacy policy, there is nothing we can do to ensure that they have done as they had promised. If they violate the commitments that they themselves had set out in their contract with us, it will fall on us, the aggrieved parties, to take the data fiduciary to court for violation of its terms of service.

Nevertheless, since consent under DEPA is provided digitally, there is an expectation that there should be some way in which we can enforce compliance more effectively. For instance, if the data fiduciary has agreed to expunge our data thirty days after it has been used, should it not be possible to programmatically ensure that this commitment is carried out? And if they say they will only use the data for a specified purpose should we not be able to prevent it from being used for anything else?

The trouble is that even under the DEPA architecture, once collected, data moves into the control of the new data fiduciary and becomes a part of its data silo. It is impossible for the data principal to have any visibility as to what is done with it from that point onwards. DEPA, in its current form, only extends to implementing consent – offering a digital interface that records that consent was provided, the purpose for which it is being sought, and the duration for which data will be retained. In its current form, there is no way for it to regulate what is done with the data after it has been collected.

Confidential Clean Rooms

That said, technology does exist to programmatically enforce this. In Europe, the Solid project, from out of the mind of the inventor of the World Wide Web, Tim Berners-Lee, aims to encase all personal data in a 'pod' and allow it to be used based on the permissioning system inherent in that layer. Users who sign up for this service will have complete control over their data since the pod always remains under their control. Data fiduciaries can ask for permission to use the data contained within the pod, and once that permission is provided, the terms of that agreement are enforced through the digital configuration of the pod. This would include shutting down access to the data in case it is used for purposes other than what was agreed. By ensuring that data remains under the control of the data principal even when it is being processed by the systems of the data fiduciary, it becomes possible to enforce use limitations on it.

However, the success of Solid depends on it being supported by the data fiduciary community, who need to configure their services to work with the data contained in these pods. At present, uptake is still slow and while it could well become a solution for the future, it is far from mainstream today. And, since a vast amount of data has already been captured and currently resides in data silos, there is little that Solid can do to address the concerns that users might legitimately have with regard to information that has already been collected.

Today, trusted computational environments exist that can guarantee that the data entrusted to them can only be processed in accordance with certain specified parameters. By incorporating these technologies into the DEPA framework, it should be possible to enforce purpose limitations and data retention obligations. Let me explain how this might be implemented.

Once consent has been obtained for the transfer of data from one data principal to another, instead of moving the data directly into the control of the new data fiduciary, the data can be placed in a confidential clean room (CCR) that has been specifically designed for that purpose. This environment is configured with full knowledge of the purpose for which the data has been collected and the algorithm that will be applied to it in order to extract the necessary inferences from it. It offers computational guarantees that data will not be processed by any algorithm other than those that meet the parameters specified and that all that will leave the clean room environment are the inferences that are extracted from the data (and not the raw data itself). Finally, it provides the assurance that once the stipulated purpose has been achieved, the raw data is expunged from the clean room.

CCRs can ensure that the raw personal data is always protected, used only for the purpose for which it was transferred and not retained any longer than absolutely necessary. As a result, it can ensure that the data is only used for the purposes for which consent was provided for its collection. And also that it does not remain within the possession of the data fiduciary for any longer than is absolutely necessary to achieve those ends.

At present, CCR development is still in an experimental phase. Questions remain as to who will operate them, what their business model should be and how the incentives of the various players in the ecosystem need to be aligned. Care needs to be taken to guard against collusion between CCR operators and those who seek to infer insights from the data contained within it. Thought must be given to where possible technological and supervisory methods may be implemented to prevent it from being misused. While much of this can be achieved if we put in place a suitable business model that addresses all these concerns by balancing the countervailing interests of the parties against each other, before it can be rolled out, we will need to establish an appropriate regulatory construct to ensure compliance.

Confidentiality and Security

Finally, it is important to ensure that the confidentiality and security of personal data in the hands of the data fiduciary is always maintained. Privacy laws impose on data fiduciaries an obligation to protect personal data against unauthorized or unlawful access or accidental loss. In other words, once they have personal data in their hands, they are obliged to ensure that this personal data does not end up in the hands of anyone who is not authorized to access it. In the unfortunate event of a data breach, most data protection laws stipulate in detail what should be done, including when the data principal needs to be informed.

All data transfers under DEPA are encrypted end-to-end. As a result, the confidentiality of the data is built into the design of the system. All transfers of data that take place through the DEPA system are completely auditable, ensuring that a paper trail is available for each data transfer. As a result, even though it is unlikely that a data breach would take place during the transfer of the data, the availability of a clear audit trail makes it possible to identify where the breach occurred and who was responsible for it.

Given that data storage under the DEPA framework is federated by design, security is implicit in its architecture. Even though it has been designed to connect previously disparate data silos, rather than to use this as an opportunity to aggregate data in one central location, DEPA leaves the data where it was stored when first collected. It is only when required further to a consent request that has been validly approved by the data principal that a small subset of that data is transferred from one data fiduciary to another.

This is a significant improvement over the way in which data portability is currently implemented. Today, under most portability systems, data fiduciaries make available to their data principals all the data under their control, allowing them to download it at one shot into a single zipped file that contains all the information that exists under the control of that data fiduciary. If this file has not been properly secured (and most of us have no idea of all that needs to be done to keep this data secure on our devices), it can be compromised, exposing the personal data contained in it to those who can misuse it in a number of different ways. Where that zipped file is then shared with any other data fiduciary – either in the process of migrating from one service to another or simply in order to share information that was previously under the control of the initial data fiduciary, it multiplies the risk of exposure as it exposes more surfaces of attack.

By design, DEPA ensures that data remains under the control (and responsibility) of the entity that first collected it. When a transfer is initiated, only that data that specifically corresponds to the request gets transferred – while all the other data remains under the control of the original data fiduciary. Where previously data transferees looked to get access to as much data as possible when given the opportunity to transfer data under their control, they are no longer under any compulsion to amass these large amounts of data, given how easy DEPA makes it to request additional information as and when required.

Since there is no restriction on the number of times that data can be requested, there is no longer any incentive to collect as much data as possible when access is provided – particularly considering the fact that the accumulation of this data will end up making the transferee liable for the consequences in the event of any breach of that data while under its control. This also makes it easier for the transferee to make the decision to delete the data once it has served the purpose for which it was transferred. Given that it is so easy to access that data again through the DEPA system, there is no real incentive to continue to keep it under their control.

Finally, once the CCR mechanism is implemented in the DEPA framework with all the necessary regulatory safeguards and institutional measures necessary to implement the technology, it will impart an additional layer of security to the data that flows through the system. Data will no longer need to be given to the requesting data fiduciary. Instead, all that needs to be done is for the data to be transferred into the CCR, from where the requesting data fiduciary can carry out the computation and extract the inferences that it needs to. What this means is that the data always remains in a secure, confidential environment without ever being commingled with all the other data under the control of the transferee. Once the computations have been carried out on the data, it is returned to the original data fiduciary or simply purged from the CCR.

Privacy Double Blind

As if this wasn't enough, DEPA offers two additional privacy safeguards that no other privacy framework can. Unlike every other framework, DEPA is techno-legal by design and its introduction of a consent manager into the data transfer workflow has offered unique opportunities to generate additional privacy features.

The first of these is a privacy double-blind that ensures that even though there are multiple parties involved in the process of the data transfer, none of them have complete knowledge of all the details of that transfer.

The consent manager is, by design, data blind. What this means is that even though data passes through the data systems managed by the consent manager as it makes its way from one data fiduciary to another, because it is encrypted end-to-end, the consent manager cannot see what data is passing through its pipes. As a result, even though the consent manager knows which data fiduciary has requested the data and which data fiduciary (or fiduciaries) are providing the data in response to the data transfer request, it has no visibility on the actual data that is sent from one to the other.

Since the data transfer request is routed through the consent manager (and not directly made of a given data fiduciary), the data fiduciary requesting the data transfer has no idea which

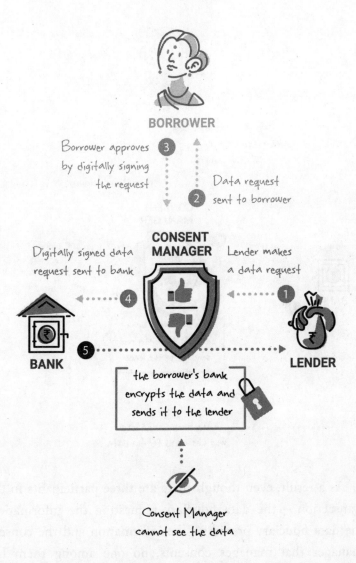

Borrower approves ③ by digitally signing the request

② Data request sent to borrower

CONSENT MANAGER

Digitally signed data request sent to bank ④

Lender makes a data request ①

BANK ⑤

the borrower's bank encrypts the data and sends it to the lender

LENDER

Consent Manager cannot see the data

data fiduciary is being asked to transfer the data. Similarly, since the transferor data fiduciary is responding to a request sent to it by the consent manager and not directly by the requesting data fiduciary, it has no visibility on which data fiduciary has made the data transfer request.

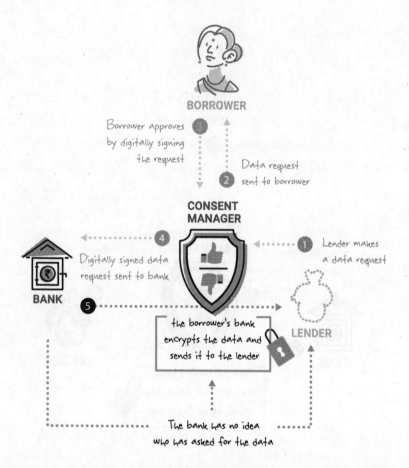

As a result, even though there are three participants in the transaction – the data fiduciary requesting the information, the data fiduciary providing the information and the consent manager that manages consents, no one among them has complete information about the transaction. This feature of DEPA imparts an additional layer of privacy protection to the data transfer architecture. By ensuring that the information signals are minimized to the maximum extent possible, it allows for additional protection beyond what is normally available.

Under what circumstances could such a feature be useful?

Let us think about a medical use case because, very often, the very nature of a medical consultation could reveal more information than the patient is comfortable disclosing. Let us imagine a scenario where a doctor with whom the patient is consulting has requested a list of medications that the patient is currently taking in order to ensure that the medicines they are about to prescribe do not react poorly with those the patient is currently taking. All the doctor has to do in a DEPA ecosystem is to make a data transfer request to the patient's consent manager requesting information about all the medicines that have been currently prescribed to the patient by anyone connected to the system. DEPA makes it possible for those who go to multiple different doctors for multiple ailments to never have to remember every drug they are taking.

Now if the patient does not want their doctor to know why they are taking that particular medicine – perhaps because they are being treated for a sexually transmitted disease or because they are embarrassed at the specific therapy they are undergoing – they are assured that the data request will only return information about the medication itself without layering on top of that any additional information about the specialization of the doctor who prescribed it. In some circumstances, that additional information is all that it would have taken to identify what ailments the data principal is suffering from – including those ailments that are the source of their embarrassment. This allows the patient to be able to provide their doctor with the required information while still ensuring an adequate level of privacy.

That said, there could be circumstances in which information about the data fiduciary that is providing this information can offer a necessary and useful signal that amplifies the quality of the data for the stated purpose. For instance, some banks are better regarded than others and the data they provide is given greater credence by others in the ecosystem. Ensuring that a potential lender is aware of the fact that the data that they are receiving has come from such a trusted bank could give them greater assurance as to its veracity and, therefore, greater confidence in granting the loan. Under these circumstances the data principal can choose to disclose the identity of the data fiduciary from which the data is being provided. This ability to invoke double-blind protection at the option of the data principal is a powerful new privacy feature that is only possible in a techno-legal data governance architecture. Allowing the data principal the opportunity to decide whether or not this additional layer of information should be disclosed or not, offers them greater autonomy over their personal data than was previously possible.

It is important to distinguish this feature from all the other data transfer systems that are being put in place around the world. Most open banking implementations that similarly allow for the transfer of data from one data fiduciary to another have not implemented an institutional consent manager along the lines of DEPA. As a result, data is sent directly from the bank in which the data is stored to the bank making the request. There is no opportunity to prevent information about the sender from being hidden from the receiver should that be desired.

While these are rarely relevant criteria in a banking scenario, I can see how it might be useful in other aspects of the financial services industry. For example, if a potential lender wants information about the net worth of a given individual, all it needs to know is the current value of the stock portfolio without information of what precise stocks are being held. The data principal should have the ability to conceal that information if required for confidentiality reasons (such as would be relevant where they are a significant shareholder in a listed entity).

Data Dashboards

One additional feature that becomes possible with the inclusion of a consent manager in the DEPA architecture is the establishment of a data dashboard that allows data principals to have a dashboard view of their transfers regardless of who is transferring the data and to whom. While this might seem like a trivial innovation, when entire ecosystems are connected in this manner, it will be incredibly valuable.

In order to appreciate just how useful this can be, let us examine a counterfactual – a system that is being deployed in Australia under its Consumer Data Rights framework. The CDR is a data-sharing architecture that, much like DEPA, was designed to share data between two data fiduciaries with the consent of the data principal. It is being implemented in the financial services sector at present but will eventually be rolled out across a range of other sectors. Data fiduciaries who have agreed to participate in the CDR framework connect their systems to each other using common protocols that will allow for mutual data sharing. If a data principal wants to share some of their data held by one bank with another bank that is also a CDR participant, all they have to do is instruct their bank to make that transfer and the data will be transferred directly from one entity to the other.

If, at a later point in time, the data principal wants to see what data they transferred, they can get a record of all their transfers from either bank. However, if they have accounts across multiple banks or, as is probably more likely, across multiple different financial sector entities that are all connected to each other on the same digital system, it is impossible for them to get information about all these transfers into a single view. They will have to go from entity to entity requesting data transfer records that will have to be manually put together into a single comprehensive view.

Since DEPA makes it possible to establish connections between all data fiduciaries and the consent managers, no matter which two entities transfer data amongst themselves, the record of each transfer is retained with the consent manager. While this may not seem that useful early in the life cycle of the ecosystem, over time, as more and more entities within a sector become capable of exchanging data with each other, this sort of single dashboard view will become invaluable.

Competition

It is by now clear that DEPA is more than just a data portability framework. Since data protection principles have been embedded into its technological design, it is effectively a governance framework for data that implements, through its technology workflows, the compliance with legal principles that have, so far, only been addressed through regulation.

But privacy is not the only area of governance that DEPA can address.

By giving data principals control over their data, DEPA has operationalized the right to data portability – elevating it from a mere right to extract data from the control of a data fiduciary to a cross-cutting framework that enables it to be used more widely. In the process, it has made it possible for data that was, for all intents and purposes, exclusively owned by the entity that collected it to be more widely used by others under the directions of the data principal.

DEPA subtly chips away at the data silos that have for so long been the source of dominance in the data economy. In a world where the mere accumulation of large data stores is seen to give data businesses a significant competitive advantage, DEPA offers us new tools with which to allow all the benefits that this might bring to be more equitably distributed amongst those who have the ability to put it to use.

The Competitiveness of Data Businesses

Competition law is designed to ensure that the benefits of a free market economy are not concentrated in the hands of only the largest businesses that operate in a given sector but that they accrue equitably to all those who participate in it. To do this, it gives regulators the tools with which to blunt any advantages that might accrue to entities that, simply because of their size or dominance in a given marketplace, can distort prices or shape consumer behaviour in their favour.

One of the remedies competition regulators can use to improve competition in the market is the power to break up entities that have grown too large. This ensures that their influence is diffused so that competition has space to develop and thrive. This has been used, in the United States of America, to restore competitiveness to various industries from time to time – iron and steel, oil, and telecom, to name a few – when each of those sectors was being dominated by one or a few dominant players. It is how competition law continues to be enforced around the world to this day.

Data has become one of the key factors of production of the modern economy. The fact that control over it lies almost exclusively in the hands of a few big companies is increasingly being seen as the latest example of competitive dominance. Regulators, the world over, are trying to figure out how best to tamp down on the harmful effects of data monopolies. In the process, they have discovered that in the data world, things work differently from the physical.

The data economy is subject to network effects that can offer considerable benefits to consumers when the market is allowed to centralize in precisely the way that competition law abhors. As a result, competition regulators who take the traditional approach and break up these dominant platforms can end up denying consumers some of the benefits that would have otherwise accrued to them.

The raison d'être of most digital commerce platforms is to provide buyers and sellers with a common digital ecosystem on which to transact their business. There are many benefits that come from digitizing the commercial process – the ability to avail services anytime and anywhere; to be able to easily compare what's on offer across a range of different brands; the fact that it solves the age-old problem of getting demand to meet supply in the most efficient way; the convenience (and affordability) that digital payments bring; and so on.

One of these advantages is the fact that it offers a single common platform on which a large number of buyers and sellers can congregate. Since buyers are always looking to be able to choose from the greatest diversity of sellers and sellers gravitate to where they can have access to the largest number of buyers, a successful digital platform is one on which the largest possible number of buyers and sellers can be aggregated in the same place.

Success, in the traditional e-commerce space, has therefore become all about consolidating towards a situation where there is one big platform to rule them all. This is what both buyers and sellers believe they need and why they are happiest when operating on the largest digital platforms. Breaking up dominant digital commerce platforms will, under these circumstances, make no one happy. And, as we have seen, given the particular way in which the technology industry is established, this is not exactly the optimal way to address competition concerns.

This, however, runs contrary to everything we already know about what it takes to foster healthy competition. We know, from past experience, that every time a market is dominated by a single commercial entity, the resulting accumulation of power distorts the ecosystem. As much as buyers and sellers might think this is what they need, unless we can dissipate the accumulated data advantage more equitably throughout the ecosystem, it will give rise to unhealthy outcomes.

This has already begun to manifest itself in the food delivery space. Complaints abound as to how the fees that these platforms charge have begun to make it impossible for restaurants to make ends meet. And since they now control so much of the demand, it is virtually impossible for food businesses to survive without them. To complicate matters, since these platforms have a bird's-eye view over what is moving and what is not, they have evolved their businesses to take advantage of this, setting up cloud kitchens that compete directly in a market in which they were supposed to provide a neutral platform. These cloud kitchens leverage the data that only they have access to in order to develop menus that are algorithmically guaranteed to consistently provide consumers with what they really want to eat. As a result, platforms become players in the games that they were originally only supposed to referee.

We need a solution that allows us to continue to avail of the benefits that network effects provide while still mitigating the harms that arise when data accumulates in a single dominant platform. While restaurants should be able to benefit from being able to use the platform to reach the largest number of customers, they should also be able to leverage network data to which their participation in the marketplace contributes in order to more accurately design their menu to provide what their customers really want.

By implementing micro data portability, DEPA offers a solution to this problem. It makes data contained in data silos more accessible, allowing it to be shared so that the advantage that exclusively vests with the original data fiduciary can be more widely utilized. While we are yet to see how this will play out in the e-commerce space, the value of this approach is already being demonstrated in the financial services space.

In that world, it is the large banks and incumbent financial services companies that have the data advantage. Since they have the largest number of consumers and the longest history of transactions, the volume of data they have to play with far exceeds anything that a new entrant in the space can hope to have.

This is a natural defence against disruption as any new business that is looking to offer new financial solutions that compete with the incumbent will not have access to the volume and granularity of data that they have. For instance, any fintech company looking to offer new innovative financial products would benefit greatly from access to data that might allow them to offer cheaper rates or more innovative structures. Without access to it, there is nothing they can do to distinguish themselves from their competitors.

Let's go back to Rajani for a moment. Having shared data about her payment history with a fintech company, she has secured a loan that she has managed to repay without defaulting. She is, as a result, eligible for future loans should she need them, having not only obtained the necessary paperwork but also – perhaps even more importantly – establishing a history of repaying her loans without defaulting on any instalment. But this last piece of information is something only the lender knows, and if it stays that way, Rajani will only ever be able to borrow from the one lender. This, in time, would lead to its own form of monopoly, one that the lenders will perpetuate, this time, thanks to the data advantage they have earned from that first interaction.

By allowing users to share data from the accounts that they have with traditional financial service providers, DEPA makes it possible for information to be accessible to new lenders. By allowing them access to information that they were previously denied, it improves the overall quality of financial services in the market and gives consumers a greater variety of service providers they can choose from. But unless the notion of data sharing extends to the new lenders as well, data monopolies will be created downstream. DEPA makes it possible to unlock this information as well. Lenders who used DEPA to access the financial information they needed are, themselves, obliged to share information as requested. As a result, other lenders can seek and obtain information about Rajani's financial discipline, which they can use to assess her eligibility for a loan – perhaps at a more preferential terms compared to what she got from the first lender.

Unlike in the brick-and-mortar world, the solution is not to break up companies that have become data monopolies. If we instead take steps to erode the data advantage implicit in the data monopoly itself, we might be able to get the best of both worlds.

DEPA allows us to make these silos more accessible, ensuring, through its technical architecture, that the data contained inside them is subject to control by the data principal. This offers new opportunities for leveraging the power and value of data without breaking up the companies that created the monopoly.

Disintermediation Benefits

One of the innovations that DEPA has introduced is the use of consent managers in the consent and data transfer workflows. While the privacy benefits of such an inclusion have been discussed in an earlier chapter, there are competitive advantages as well.

In a world without DEPA, the only way to set up a data transfer arrangement between two data fiduciaries would be to have the transferor and transferee entities work together to make sure that their respective technical infrastructures are compatible with each other so that information sent by one could easily be received by the other. This is what most jurisdictions (the UK and Australia, for example) that are seeking to implement open data frameworks have done. In these countries, the regulators have set out the broad protocols and technical frameworks underpinning these transfer arrangements but have left it to the individual data fiduciaries to work out how their systems will actually integrate with each other.

The problem with leaving it to the data fiduciaries to agree to transfer arrangements amongst themselves is that there is nothing to stop them from colluding to establish preferential arrangements. This could result in the larger, more established players banding together to set up arrangements between themselves that are designed to perpetuate their data advantage while strategically excluding newer entrants. Since every entity is free to bilaterally enter into data transfer arrangements with every other entity, there is no way to ensure all the entities within the ecosystem function in accordance with a uniform set of terms and conditions.

Instead of mitigating the incumbents' data advantage, this could perpetuate it.

By introducing a third party into the data transfer workflow, DEPA ensures that all data fiduciaries are subject to the same data transfer obligations. In such a situation, data fiduciaries do not connect to each other bilaterally. Instead, when they sign up to the ecosystem, all they have to do is make sure their systems can connect to a consent manager, and, since the consent manager is capable of connecting to the other data fiduciaries, the new data fiduciary is automatically capable of porting data to and from every other data fiduciary on the system. This eliminates the need for bilateral arrangements (which, in an ecosystem with many data fiduciaries, could end up being an extremely challenging exercise) and also ensures that every entity participating in the ecosystem is doing so by remaining in compliance with the same set of terms and conditions.

By unbundling personal data transfer workflows into their constituent elements – (i) consent flows and (ii) data flows – DEPA has made it possible to implement a scalable data transfer system that new data fiduciaries can join at any time without having to bilaterally engage with all the existing participants in the ecosystem. While this has been achieved through the design of the technology infrastructure, similar efforts have gone into creating the legal agreement (the ecosystem participation terms) that all participants in the ecosystem need to adhere to.

Operationalization of DPI

'Individual commitment to a group effort – that is what makes a team work, a company work, a society work, a civilization work.'
– Vince Lombardi

We've seen how regulatory principles can be implicitly embedded into the design of DPI so that regulators and systems engineers can shape the behaviour of market participants in a manner that is aligned with policy objectives. We've also seen how legislative objectives can be coded into the architecture so that any infrastructure that is digital from end to end can be designed so that the mere act of participating in the ecosystem ensures compliance with legislative imperatives.

But even though these systems are digital at the core, they are designed to interact with market participants. They are, as a result, liable to being captured – either by aggressive and unchecked market forces or unconstrained regulation. In order to protect the ecosystem against distortions caused by these exogenous factors, we must also address these risks in the overall design of the ecosystem.

There are, broadly speaking, three types of ecosystem participants – the government, non-profit organizations and the private sector. In different configurations, they are the main actors in India's digital public infrastructure. Each of them responds to various incentives. We need to understand these different considerations so that the roles assigned to each of them appropriately array the positive incentives of one against the negative incentives of the other. By carefully balancing countervailing forces in this manner, it should be possible to align the overall ecosystem in the direction of the desired outcome.

Let us now analyse the roles that each of these categories of market participants needs to play in the ecosystem and how they can be arrayed against each other to ensure that all the incentives are appropriately aligned.

The Role of the Government

The government is a core participant in the digital public infrastructure. In many instances, its involvement derives from the sovereign functions it is required to perform – both as a regulator as well as an active participant. In many instances, it plays a coordinating role in providing the relevant level of assurance to new entrants that the system is functioning under the guidance of the government.

One way to evaluate the extent of the government's involvement in a given digital public infrastructure would be to determine how closely the functional objectives of that DPI are identified with the government's sovereign function. For instance, a government-issued unique identity is often seen as an essential requirement for the provision of government services, subsidies and benefits. As a result, it tends to be strongly correlated with the government's sovereign duty to its citizens. The provision of this service should, as a result, not be delegated. Any digital public infrastructure that provides identity services – from the actual issuance of the unique identity to the various features associated with the digital identity such as authentication, KYC, etc. – would therefore need to have a high level of government involvement.

On the other hand, digital infrastructure for electronic commerce – particularly where all it does is establish a set of common protocols that market participants (sellers, buyers and everyone in between) need to conform to, has nothing to do with the sovereign functions of the State. Examples abound of these sorts of marketplaces today – both offline as well as online. The government plays no role in them when they exist entirely in an offline format, and there is no reason to expect that it needs to when they are transformed into digital ecosystems. At best, the role the government could play is to authorize a given protocol in order to provide an assurance of neutrality that no private platform can offer.

Apart from very few instances where the digital infrastructure performs a role akin to a sovereign function, the government usually functions as a neutral party whose involvement in the ecosystem gives private participants comfort that none of their competitors can gain an unfair advantage by choosing protocols and specifications that are self-preferencing.

On the other hand, while digital infrastructure is, for the most part, far less expensive to deploy than physical infrastructure, the cost of building population-scale systems is not insignificant. Particularly when it comes to foundational infrastructure, the resources required to deploy them could sometimes be beyond the capacity of private enterprise to absorb. In these instances, it is impossible for anyone other than a governmental entity to garner the resources – financial and otherwise – to pull this off.

There are many reasons why the government should not be involved in the development of digital systems. In the first place, governments have never had any incentive to develop new cutting-edge solutions and therefore lack the experience required to do so. There is enough evidence of this in the various digitization projects that government entities have undertaken by themselves – all of which tend to be suboptimal both in terms of innovation in the design of the solution and in their experience of using it.

It is also fair to say that, in certain areas, trust in the government and the neutrality with which it operates is ebbing. This is particularly true when the state has the discretion to prefer certain private entities over others in commercial transactions – such as, for instance when the project to deploy critical hardware and software elements of the infrastructure is awarded to one private sector entity over others.

There are also concerns that the government's ability to access the data residing in or flowing through these digital systems may eventually be shared with other government entities and used for the purpose of surveillance or other investigative and law enforcement purposes. If digital infrastructure that has a bearing on these issues is implemented without due process, trust in digital ecosystems will falter. The fact that all of government is viewed as a single monolithic institution despite the many ministries and departments it is actually composed of adds to this perception.

Wherever possible, care must be taken to ensure that the issues listed above are adequately addressed in the design of digital infrastructure. While we can create standard operating procedures and internal operating guidelines that prescribe how the government should behave, it would be far better to establish systemic measures that achieve this balance outside of regulation.

What Can the Private Sector Do?

The biggest and most obvious advantage the private sector has over the public sector is its capacity for innovation and its ability to constantly find new ways to reach the end consumer. Private enterprise exists to find innovative solutions to market problems and we need to harness this capacity to also solve societal problems.

Take consumer outreach. Since the private sector is motivated by commercial gain, so long as they can be shown what's in it for them, they will willingly deploy vast armies of motivated resources to proliferate the solution deep into the target population. Nothing tops healthy competition between adequately motivated private players, and if they can be arrayed against each other in an appropriately competitive environment, we can achieve far better results than if we looked to the government to roll it out.

Having said that said, it is important to ensure that these overriding commercial imperatives do not result in outcomes that are not in the public interest. As much as the involvement of the private sector can ensure that these ecosystems remain innovative and stay current in response to evolutions in technology, they should not be allowed to establish and entrench monopolistic advantages. For instance, even if the ecosystem has been designed so that multiple private entities are allowed to participate in the provision of the service, care should be taken to ensure that the largest among them do not create a cartel to collectively gain an unfair advantage.

It is also important to ensure that there is sufficient diversity of private participants in the ecosystem so that the success of the digital public infrastructure doesn't rest on the continued viability of a single or even a few market participants. While India's payment systems have a vast number of participants, close to 85 per cent of the entire market for digital payment is under the control of two private entities. The Indian payment regulator and the central bank tried to impose restrictions on the ecosystem that would result in no one entity processing more than 33 per cent of all digital payment transactions.

That proposal did not, eventually, go through – largely in tacit acknowledgement of the fact that ecosystems such as these are capital intensive, requiring long periods of investment with little expectation of profit. Until there is evidence that private players in the space are not acting in a manner that unfairly prejudices consumers, any intervention in anticipation of future anticompetitive effects is meaningless. What's more, digital businesses have shown that with greater market concentration, it is possible to generate network effects that are of considerable benefit to consumers.

As we think about the role of the private sector in digital public ecosystems, these are the considerations we need to weigh. On the one hand, we need to ensure that there is adequate competition in the markets, putting in place appropriate measures to prevent players from abusing their position of dominance. At the same time, we need to acknowledge that in some of these sectors, it will be impossible to see a multiplicity of participants with roughly similar market share.

Non-Profit Self-Regulatory Organizations

There would have been no need for a third category of market player had we not needed an intermediate entity to act as a foil between the other two.

Where the government does not have the technical capabilities to develop necessary protocols and specifications, we cannot simply hand the responsibility for this over to the private sector and expect them to forsake shareholder profits in the public interest. The success of digital public infrastructure depends heavily on the common technological underpinnings of the ecosystem. These are the protocols on which client-facing applications are built and to which the plumbing required to connect market participants with each other needs to conform. At the same time, we cannot hand over to private technology companies the responsibility of building these protocols without running the risk of capture.

To mitigate this, we need to vest the responsibility of creating these protocols with a neutral entity and make them responsible for not just creating the standards but also ensuring that they are constantly updated.

Non-profit organizations can provide the technical capabilities needed to develop and maintain the standards and protocols according to which these digital public infrastructure function. Since they will not be constrained in the way government entities are, they will have the freedom to hire and maintain an appropriately trained staff. Since they are established as non-profit entities, their organizational objectives will not be constrained by the need to generate a return on shareholder investment – and subsequently limit the types of activities that they can undertake.

In order to adequately represent the interests of all the entities within the ecosystem, it is important to ensure that all categories of market participants have a say. In addition, it is important to develop appropriate governance mechanisms that protect the interests of stakeholders, as well as further the overall objectives for which the digital public infrastructure was established. To achieve this, it is important to suppress the commercial advantages that some market participants might obtain in the short term in the interests of the longer-term objective of ensuring the success of the entire ecosystem.

This is a model that has been successfully deployed globally. Around the world, there are three main technical standards organizations that determine the way in which new standards are determined and deployed – the IEEE (the Institute of Electrical and Electronics Engineers), the IETF (the Internet Engineering Task Force) and W3C (the World Wide Web Consortium). While they each are constituted differently with their own unique governance models, there is much we can learn from how they function as we look to deploy this in a domestic context.

There are other circumstances under which non-profit organizations such as these can be useful. Since investments in private enterprise always come with an expectation that these investments will generate a return, there is an obligation to show results – often within a short and predictable time horizon. Each project into which an entity invests time and resources needs to be able to justify that investment on the basis of an easily identifiable and achievable outcome.

The impact that digital public infrastructure will have is often not evident at inception. In most instances, the solutions they are implementing break new ground, requiring traditional workflows to be unbundled and reimagined with brand-new solutions that exist completely outside the existing frame of reference. It is not easy for private entities who are primarily answerable to their shareholders to take the leap of faith required in order to roll out these projects.

Non-profit organizations have no obligation to demonstrate to their shareholders a commercial return on investment. As a result, they can be tasked with building out initial proofs-of-concept that, if these solutions end up being successful, will serve as a demonstration of the potential that this new pathway holds. This, in turn, could be used to convince shareholders of private enterprises that might have been sitting on the fence that investing in this space would be worthwhile.

Most countries have leveraged the infrastructure provided by card networks to serve as the rails for digital payment solutions. India chose a different path. It chose to leverage the IMPS network that was already functioning between most large banks in the country. When UPI was first launched, it was not immediately evident that this new method of digital payments was going to be successful.

In order to catalyse adoption, the National Payments Corporation of India (a non-profit organization owned by a wide range of Indian commercial banks that had been set up with the objective of organizing the digital payments space within the country) developed the BHIM app and launched it in on 30 December 2016. As the first consumer-facing digital application that offered UPI payments, this was the proof of concept that eventually catalysed enough industry interest in this new model of digital payments to encourage private sector enterprises like Google Pay and PhonePe to invest in the space. While those two companies account for close to 85 per cent of the digital payment market share today, they may never have considered committing to UPI had they not been able to study the BHIM experience.

To summarize, there are three categories of participants in digital ecosystems – government, private enterprise and non-profit entities. Each of these three categories has different objectives. As a result, they each respond to different incentives. In order to achieve optimal outcomes, the operationalization of digital public infrastructure must take into account these factors and optimally allocate responsibility among these different participants in such a manner as to ensure that these various incentives are arrayed against each other in a way that achieves the desired results.

We need to evaluate these considerations and try and illustrate how the different objectives sought to be achieved can be implemented across the many different phases of the development of these DPI.

The Design Phase

The design of DPI is a technical exercise that calls for an innovative approach to problem-solving. It involves more than merely overlaying digital processes over traditional workflows. This expertise does not lie with the government, which prefers to stick to tried and tested models that have had a long history of success. While it is possible for the government to develop technical expertise (and, in fact, many departments of the government have done so), it is hard for them to shake this path dependency and build the kind of innovation muscle necessary to generate the sorts of solutions that are required. For these reasons, it is probably inadvisable to leave it to the government to design new digital public infrastructure solutions.

Private sector companies are similarly unsuitable considering the long-term implications of their participation in the DPI. Anyone who has been involved in the design of the infrastructure could be perceived to have obtained an advantage by being privy to information about how these systems function.

For these reasons, the entities ideally suited to work on the conceptualization and design of these systems are non-profit technical standards organizations. These entities have the inherent technical capabilities required in order to be able to design technology solutions. They would be ideally suited to working on the conceptualization and implementation of these systems.

That said, care should be taken to ensure that these organizations are not 'captured' by the private sector. Since they are non-profit entities by their charter, they remain dependent on external sources for their funding. Unless we ensure that this does not happen, it is possible – likely even – that their donors will determine the directional outcomes of their work. We must ensure, through appropriate regulation if need be, that these donors cannot influence outcomes in such a manner that their products and standards are incorporated into the design of the ecosystem in ways that secure for them a disproportionate advantage. We can, by way of illustration, look at how the NPCI has been organized. It has been set up as a not-for-profit company with its shareholding split between sixty-five banks and fintech companies – representing the financial ecosystem it has been built to manage.

In summary, care must be taken to ensure that the private sector is not involved in the design of digital public infrastructure in a manner that will allow any additional advantage to accrue to them. In an ideal world, these systems should be designed by the public sector, but considering how ill-equipped the public sector is when it comes to the design and development of technology solutions, they are singularly unsuitable for carrying out all of the conceptualization and implementation. The preferred role of the government would be to select a design solution from among those conceived of and presented by neutral non-profit think tanks and to similarly be involved in the continuing evolution of the standards implicit in the deployment of these solutions.

The Proliferation Phase

Once designed, the digital public infrastructure needs to be deployed in the market and allowed to proliferate. This is what the private sector excels at. They know exactly how to design technology so that it can be easily consumed – even by unsophisticated first-time users. They have the human resources and organization capabilities to deploy the boots on the ground that are necessary in order to extend digital public infrastructure to the furthest reaches of the country. With the right commercial incentives, the private sector can ensure that the digital public infrastructure proliferates deep into its intended market. What's more, the same commercial incentives can ensure a constantly improving user experience for customers.

That said, care must be taken to ensure that as a result of allowing private participation, no one entity is able to assume a dominant position in the market. It is important to ensure that the ecosystem is designed to enable multiple private sector parties to become involved in the development and deployment of the ecosystem. Enabling adequate competition among the private sector participants will ensure a diversity of options and the availability of a wide range of products and services. Carefully calibrating the extent of the market share a single private sector participant can acquire will further ensure that the ecosystem remains healthy and the end user benefits.

It is often difficult to convince the private sector to make the required investment into a new digital public infrastructure that is breaking new ground. There is often no precedent and outcomes are uncertain. For private companies accountable to their shareholders, this often represents an unacceptable risk. In order to give private companies the confidence to invest in these ecosystems, it is often necessary to create a proof of concept so that they can visualize the benefits that can accrue from their participation in the deployment of these ecosystems. The government can either fund the development of these proofs of concept or lean on non-profit entities to do so. In India, the government's funding of the BHIM app, which has been discussed before, is a case in point.

Finally, there are certain categories of digital public infrastructure that fall so squarely within the remit of the state that care should be taken to ensure that the role of the private sector is limited to the maximum extent possible. The deployment of the Aadhaar identity programme is a case in point.

The organization that is responsible for the management of Aadhaar is the Unique Identity Authority of India, a statutory authority established under the provisions of the Aadhaar Act 2016. While the core infrastructure remains exclusively in the hands of the Authority – that not only manages the identity repository in which biometric and demographic information is stored but is also responsible for other aspects, including the evolution of the digital standards – the responsibility for enrolment of citizens across the length and breadth of the country was subcontracted to various private entities. In order to retain control over the process, they were subject to strict conditions and controls. All enrolment agents were required to input their biometrics before enrolling each new candidate, ensuring that they were accountable for their actions of onboarding these entities and, more importantly, to ensure that should any malfeasance be detected, the enrolment agent who was responsible for this could be brought to book.

Furthermore, in order to ensure the most efficient and effective deduplication algorithms were being deployed on the enrolment data that was being processed, the government engaged the services of three private sector players to process enrolment data. By playing them off against each other by carefully crafting the incentives to ensure that they were each looking to innovate in the solutions that they developed for the overall benefit of the ecosystem.

To summarize, the proliferation and deployment of new digital public infrastructure is best carried out by the private sector, which has both the human resources as well as the appetite for innovation that is required in order to acquire consumers of the service. However, care must be taken to ensure that this access does not result in a given private player assuming market dominance that would harm the public. It is also important to ensure that the government or the regulator has adequate control over the manner in which the private sector operates in order to ensure that there is no capture. This can be ensured both through technical and operational measures as well as through the implementation of regulatory frameworks.

The Governance Phase

The final element in the operationalization of digital public infrastructure has to do with its long-term governance. It is one thing to conceptualize and design the digital infrastructure. It is a completely different thing to deploy it in such a way that ensures that it continues to function in a manner that is responsive to the requirements of its stakeholders as well as of evolving regulatory and technological requirements. This calls for active governance that requires specific organizational, legal and regulatory measures.

Before getting into a deeper discussion on the modalities of governance, it is important to place the governance of these systems within the overall regulatory framework. Since most digital public infrastructure impinges upon sovereign functions, the sectors they operate are often regulated.

There is, as a result, a need to fit these new digital models into existing legislative frameworks. Where the digital public infrastructure is just a means to implement that which has been permitted under a law, their use can be authorized through the enactment of rules and regulations. Where there is no such authorization, the existing law would need to be amended or a new law enacted. Once so authorized, the digital public infrastructure will be governed by the stipulations set out in that legislative instrument. Any technical or organizational measures that are put in place must operate within the stipulations contained in that law.

In thinking about the governance of the digital public infrastructure, there are three clear framings within which the discussion should revolve: (i) the governance of the operations of the digital infrastructure, (ii) the governance of the technical standards and its future evolution and (iii) the governance of the stakeholders. Let us examine each of them separately.

The Operation of the DPI

At the core of all digital public infrastructure are a set of technical and operational activities that are essential to its operation. This includes, where relevant, the operation of a central switch to which the various stakeholders have to connect their respective systems; the certification of the ecosystem participants to confirm that they comply with the requirements of the protocol before they are allowed to go live on the system; the implementation, where necessary of a hierarchy of permissioning and authorization so that all the ecosystem participants have a level of access to the ecosystem that is appropriate to their role in the ecosystem.

Since these decisions can favour one or the other participant in the ecosystem, it is critical that the power to take these decisions be vested in entities that are demonstrably neutral. This rules out private players who have a lot to gain if they give preference to allied entities over competitors. Ideally, this is a role that the government should play, considering that it would, in such ecosystems, be seen as a neutral regulator of market activities. Where the government is unable to manage complex technology systems itself, it should either build the capacity internally or outsource the management to third parties under its control.

Another alternative would be to establish self-regulatory organizations in which there is both representation of the members of the ecosystem as well as participation by the government regulator. This would ensure that the government remains one level removed from the day-to-day operations of the core functions of the digital public infrastructure while still retaining a handle on it in order to ensure that decisions are not being taken by the ecosystem participants in a manner that would unfairly prejudice the end-users. One way to mitigate those concerns would be to ensure that there is a diversity of viewpoints on the board – by ensuring that the widest possible selection of ecosystem participants is made part of the governance of the self-regulatory organization.

Governance of Technical Standards

The next element of governance revolves around the development of the technical standards and their ongoing evolution. Since DPI implements in code various regulatory objectives, it presents an opportunity to reflect ideals of governance into the code. In order to achieve that objective, it is important to ensure that the correct principles are reflected in the protocols and standards that describe this infrastructure. Well-defined protocols that embed into them regulatory principles will help shape behaviour in the ecosystem and will ensure compliance with the overall regulatory objectives in a far better manner than could have been achieved by regulation alone. When implemented in code, compliance with the regulatory requirements is assured by merely participating in the ecosystem.

Since these protocols will determine how these ecosystems are designed and operated, it is important to ensure that they are neutral in terms of the benefit they bestow on various market participants. If the private sector is involved in developing the standards and protocols, there is a risk that they might influence the design so that they can gain commercial advantage out of them. On the other hand, since governments are not particularly good at building out technology systems, it would not make sense to devolve the responsibility for these standards on the government. Neutral technical standards organizations that are not owned or controlled by private sector entities could be tasked with the responsibility of both building the initial protocols as well as managing all evolutions based on new technology requirements or changes in regulation.

In order to ensure neutrality, it might be important to allow a multiplicity of such technical standards organizations to develop and present proposals for the standards to be adopted. The government could then make a subjective decision on which protocols to adopt and allow the organization that proposed it to be responsible for the initial specification. However, for all evolutions of the standard, the government should be free to seek proposals from the larger ecosystem in order to ensure that as wide a range of options and considerations are presented. While this would ensure that the standards truly develop in a democratic manner, we must take care to ensure that we do not sacrifice efficiency and efficacy at the altar of democracy.

Stakeholder Governance

The final leg of the governance piece has to do with establishing the frameworks for how the various non-government participants in the ecosystem must behave. While the protocols will, to a large extent, determine how the system functions (including, if it is carefully designed, how the regulatory principles will be embedded into the technical architecture), there is almost as much that happens outside of the technology architecture as within. For instance, we need appropriate mechanisms for the enforcement of legal obligations and the establishment and operation of dispute resolution frameworks. It is important that we pay as much care and attention to these aspects of the ecosystem as we do to the operational and technology design.

That said, since these ecosystems are largely digital, it should be possible to optimize these governance solutions by leveraging the technology underpinnings of the infrastructure. Take dispute resolution, for example. Given that these digital ecosystems have been designed to carry out high-velocity transactions at population-scale, it would be a shame if that is set at naught simply because of inefficiencies in the dispute resolution process. Which is why, instead of referring disputes to the traditional court system or even to arbitration and mediation, many Indian

DPIs have chosen online dispute resolution. Not only does this do away with the need for all parties to the dispute to be physically present in the same location as the adjudicator, it could, if the adjudicator is so inclined, also allow the adjudication to proceed largely asynchronously based solely on the written submissions of the parties.

There are other ways in which the fact that these systems are digital from end to end could be leveraged to improve dispute resolution outcomes. For instance, it should be possible, from a review of the dashboards, audit logs and record-keeping systems that form part of these systems, to incontrovertibly establish what exactly went wrong with a disputed transaction and which party was to blame. This is all the evidence that any adjudicator would need to apportion liability between the disputing parties. That said, care must be taken to ensure that any such digital evidence is irrefutable and the logs within which it is contained are demonstrably tamper-proof.

Another important aspect of stakeholder governance is the establishment of an appropriate contractual framework that sets out the rights and obligations of the respective participants in the ecosystem and documents their roles and corresponding obligations. It is only on the basis of such a document that liability can be apportioned and obligations enforced. Many of India's DPI ecosystems have put in place non-profit, self-regulatory organizations to coordinate the execution of these agreements by new entrants, their certification as being fit to participate in the ecosystem and their subsequent supervision in the interests of the overall health of the ecosystem. These self-regulatory organizations are responsible for the maintenance of the DPI ecosystem and the management of its various stakeholders on a day-to-day basis.

It is only if a digital ecosystem has all these elements in place that it will be able to mature and grow.

The DPI Approach to Governance

'In cyberspace, we must understand how a different "code" regulates – how the software and hardware (i.e., the "code" of cyberspace) that make cyberspace what it is, also regulate cyberspace as it is.'

– Lawrence Lessig

Our initial instinct was correct. Market forces can be leveraged to keep the technology industry in check. But in order to do that, we need to first create the playground in which these private enterprises can play. We need to do this the old-fashioned way – by designing protocols within which they are constrained to operate. This allows us to create appropriately constrained environments within which private sector entities can compete with each other to deliver services while still being held in check by the limits of what the protocol allows them to do.

This is a new approach to governance – one that embeds legal principles into the technology architecture so that the rules according to which participants have to play are embedded into the design of the ecosystem in which they are operating.

There are inherent advantages to this. By embedding policy objectives into protocol design, regulators have much more direct control over the actions of those they regulate. They can make policy changes by altering the protocol and immediately see the effects of their decision reflected in the market. Private participants, for their part, will get the sort of clarity they lacked when they had to comply with the letter of the law. Laws expressed in words are subject to interpretation, and companies could stretch these to mean one thing while regulators (and eventually courts) could interpret such laws to mean something else.

Code is unambiguous. When we express policy as code, market participants are left with no doubt as to what they can or cannot do. They are free to innovate in every which way they choose so long as the protocol permits it. But if anything they want to do does not align with what the protocol allows, there is no way they can interpret their way out of it.

While technology companies may no longer get to decide how the market needs to operate, they retain enough flexibility in operations to allow them to continue to innovate in new directions. This should allow them to continue to profit from participating in the ecosystem. If some of their innovations end up being too extreme, taking the market in directions that regulators do not want it to go or placing consumers at any sort of risk, it is possible for regulators to gently place their thumb on the scale by making suitable alterations to the protocol to prevent them from going down that path.

There are technical and operational measures that need to be put in place in order to implement this approach. Regulators will have to upgrade their capabilities so that they can effectively use these new tools they have been given. New neutral institutions will need to be set up to fill in the gaps in organizational design to ensure that appropriate checks and balances are in place.

While the approach has been implemented in some regulated sectors in India – finance and health, among others, the principles that underpin this approach have broad applicability. They can just as easily be applied in other sectors where the infrastructure has been designed to be digital from end to end. That said, there are areas where this is not an appropriate approach for regulation, sectors like defence, energy, telecom and space, which are either not yet ripe for digital disruption or where the outcomes required cannot be appropriately achieved through this protocol-based approach. Regulators need to be able to assess this for themselves, identifying those sectors where this approach will work and where it will not in order to be most effective.

At the end of the day, it all comes down to design. So far, the focus has been on the technology. The architects of India's digital ecosystems have focused solely on the technical aspects of the design of these systems. They have, in the process, created frameworks that incorporate principles of data protection and which promote competition that has laid the foundations for this new regulatory approach that we can now see is possible.

But this is just a start. In order to carry this forward, we will need to embed regulations in the code with much more nuance and purpose. This will call for multistakeholder participation in the design process. Where it was sufficient to have technologists lead the design process, it is increasingly going to be important to involve regulators, lawyers and policy professionals. Each of them will need to learn the language of the other – lawyers and policy professionals will need to be able to understand all that technology is capable of so that they know the extent to which their policy considerations can be incorporated into code and what is possible to be achieved through technology. Technologists, for their part, need to appreciate policy imperatives so that they can devise new technology artefacts that can give life to these regulatory objectives.

We have seen when it comes to governance that neither the US's laissez-faire approach nor Europe's regulation-heavy approach has been particularly effective. On the other hand, DPI, if properly designed, can offer a third way – an approach to data governance that strikes a balance between the two approaches that currently exist, presenting benefits to both regulators and entrepreneurs. It allows policymakers to embed regulatory principles directly into the code of the digital ecosystems that they govern so that private parties can freely innovate within constraints imposed by code.

The future of technology regulation is techno-legal.

And it is already here.

Acknowledgements

In December 2022, I had dinner with Nandan Nilekani at Manu Chandra's test kitchen in Bengaluru. Over several courses of superlative food and wine, we hit upon the idea of writing a book about India's digital public infrastructure (DPI) and the fact that it was not just a technology solution for development but a completely new approach to data governance. I had already been writing about this idea in my weekly column in the *Mint*, and Nandan felt it was time to present these ideas more fully in a book. His only caveat was that whatever I did, I had to get it out soon because the time was ripe for something like this.

Nandan is the fulcrum around which the DPI movement, in India for over a decade and a half and now across the rest of the world, revolves. He is an inspiration, and I am extraordinarily privileged to have had the opportunity to work with him and have him for a sounding board for much of my thinking on these nuanced issues.

As far as the actual ideas in this book are concerned, they emerged, as is often the case, out of many, many conversations over the years with various people associated with the DPI ecosystem. I can't list each contribution, so I am going to list in alphabetical order all those I can recall, recognizing that even while doing so, there may be many I have omitted to mention: Arun Sukumar, B.G. Mahesh, C.V. Madhukar, Hrushi Mehta, Kamya Chandra, Meghana Reddyreddy, Nikhil Kumar, Pramod Varma, Pramod Rao, Sachin Malhan, Sanjay Jain, Saurabh Karn, Saurabh Panjwani, Sharad Sharma, Siddharth Shetty, Siddharth Tiwari, Sujith Nair, Supriya Sankaran, T. Koshy, Tanuj Bhojwani and Vivek Raghavan. Thank you all for all the conversations and for helping create this book.

Much of my thinking has been sharpened while writing papers on the many topics in this book. Through writing, researching and engaging with co-authors and peer reviewers, I've been forced to be more precise about what I am saying and present my ideas in more universally understood ways. Among these, probably the most significant papers were those I contributed to, along with Siddharth Tiwari, Frank Packer and Derryl D'Silva, which forced me to think about data governance in the global context. Also noteworthy was the paper I wrote with Prakhar Misra and Harshita Agarwal on how these ecosystems are funded and the incentives we need to be mindful of. Most recently, the article I wrote with Rudra Chaudhuri and Keyzom Ngodup helped me step back and look at the DPI approach holistically and in a broader context.

And there is my column in the *Mint*, which I have written since 2016. The weekly exercise of cranking out 950 words on the intersection of law and technology has given me a platform to dig deeply into minor issues or, if I so choose, to zoom out and take a broader perspective. There is no better way to test out a grand argument than in public, week after week.

I've been fortunate to have had access to key individuals at the

helm of some of the most influential organizations at the heart
of India's DPI story. They have been most generous with their
time, explaining the finer points of the systems they operate and
sharing with me the challenges they have faced in building India's
digital infrastructure into what it is. I am particularly grateful
to Dr Ram Sewak Sharma, with whom I interacted when he
was at the Unique Identification Authority of India (UIDAI),
then the Telecom Regulatory Authority of India (TRAI) and
finally at the National Health Authority (NHA); Dilip Asbe
from National Payments Corporation of India (NPCI); Saurabh
Garg from the UIDAI; and Abhishek Singh, of the National
eGovernance Division of the Government of India.

In the run-up to and throughout India's G20 Presidency, I
worked closely with the Ministry of Finance to shape India's key
priorities. I was fortunate to have been appointed DPI Advisor
to the Ministry of Finance, contributing, in my small way, to
developing India's DPI priorities under the Global Partnership
for Financial Inclusion Track. Much of this book was written
while I was helping with that work and, as a result, has been
significantly shaped by the many conversations I have had
with Ajay Seth (Secretary, Department of Economic Affairs),
V. Anantha Nageswaran (Chief Economic Advisor to the
Government of India), Chanchal Sarkar (Global Partnership for
Financial Inclusion [GPFI] Co-chair), Monica Thind, Harsha
Bhoumik and the entire (tireless) team from the Ministry
of Finance.

I must particularly acknowledge the two other DPI advisors
to the Ministry of Finance, Kamya Chandra and Siddharth
Shetty, along with whom so much of my contribution to India's
DPI agenda has taken place. Almost all of this book was written

while we figured out how to present critical concepts to various stakeholders. As a result, it has benefitted immeasurably from extended conversations about how these complex ideas could be explained in the most accessible way. The Ministry of Finance might have concatenated our initials for convenience, but we were so tickled by the superstardom implicit in the acronym 'SRK' that we wore it as a badge of honour.

Various think tanks in India and abroad were kind enough to create the space for conversations around DPI. This is where many of the ideas in this book had room to evolve and grow. I must point out, in particular, the Carnegie Endowment for International Peace, which seized on the idea of DPI and used its convening power – both in India and the US – to discuss it on the global stage. I must mention, in particular, the tireless efforts of Rudra Chaudhury and the entire team of Carnegie India, who organized events and meetings with so many people in India and abroad, that allowed the notion of DPI to reach more ears than would otherwise have been possible.

I shared excerpts and early versions of the book with many people whose opinions I value. I am grateful to them for agreeing to read a book that was still far from done and sending me comments on how to make it better. I would particularly like to thank C.V. Madhukar, who ploughed through a very, very early draft of my big argument and, over a long walk in Washington D.C., took me through the ways in which I could improve it. I also owe a deep debt of gratitude to Meghana Reddyreddy, who trawled through, not just one but two versions of the draft. Her detailed comments forced me to rethink how I was presenting key concepts in the book and to include others I had inadvertently skipped. Meghana and I have worked in the trenches to deploy many of the techno-legal concepts discussed for the first time in this book. There is no one I trust more to hold my feet to the fire than her.

I would also like to thank Amitabh Kant and Nandan Nilekani (who together constitute India's high-level task force on Digital Public Infrastructure) for taking the time out of their busy schedules to read this book and write the endorsements you will find on the back cover. It is thanks to the tireless work of these two gentlemen that the term DPI has come to be so widely accepted around the world. I must also thank Justice B.N. Srikrishna, who immediately responded to my request to read a near-final draft despite being on vacation with his grandson. His endorsement of the ideas in these pages mean more to me than he will know.

Chiki Sarkar agreed to publish this book after just one meeting and a cursory read of an early draft. Her detailed comments pushed me to make it better and include sections I had thought were unnecessary. I am also grateful to Devangshu Datta, my indefatigable editor, for all the tough love with the edits. We had so many arguments over the shape of the book that there were times I was convinced I should just walk away. I am glad I didn't because the book is better for the additional work I put in. Authors tend to confuse knowledge of the subject matter with an appreciation of what readers would like to read. It takes a good publisher and editor to gently disabuse them of these notions.

My mother has always been a silent supporter of everything I do. This time, instead of waiting for the finished copy, she took it upon herself to read an early version of the book, painstakingly making handwritten notes of all the typos and spelling mistakes.

She assured me that she had understood every word I wrote and that if she could, anyone would. The one difference between this book and the last is that my father is no longer with us. My dad was never one to make a big deal of anything I did or wrote. But I miss his silent approval.

These projects take the greatest toll on my wife Ahalya and my son Dhruv who have had to put up with me being mentally absent for months until I was done.

I wish I could say this is the last of it, but by now they know better.

A Note on the Author

Rahul Matthan heads the technology practice at the law firm Trilegal, where he is a partner. His work on the governance of India's digital public infrastructure includes advising regulators like the UIDAI, NPCI and NHA. He has assisted the Government of India in developing its DPI priorities as part of its G20 Presidency and he serves as a DPI Advisor to the Ministry of Finance. He has also served as a member of the Technology Sub-Committee of the Reserve Bank of India's Committee on Household Finance, as well as being a member of the Kris Gopalakrishnan committee on Non-Personal Data. Since 2016, he has written a weekly column in the *Mint* called 'Ex Machina', which deals with issues at the intersection of technology, law and society. His podcast by the same name, covers similar ground.